English Code 4

Student's Book

Contents

Unit	Unit aims	Vocabulary and Phonics	Values
Welcome back! pp. 4–9	How can I talk about myself? • Describe vacations. • Describe family. • Use dates. • Ask and answer about birthdays.	**Family:** aunt, uncle, grandparent, parent **Ordinal numbers:** 1st–31st	Listen to others and say how you feel.
1 Into the wild pp. 10–23	How can we plan a class adventure? • Use outdoor activity words. • Talk about future plans using *going to*. • Ask and answer about future plans. • Write an SOS message.	**Outdoor activity words:** compass, gloves, map, matches, rope, boots, whistle, wheel, blanket, branches, leaves, grass **Phonics:** ir, ear bird, girl, search, heard	Work together.
2 Into the past pp. 24–37	How can I make a model of an Aztec city? • Use words to describe life in the past. • Compare the past and present. • Ask and answer using *could* and *ago*. • Write a newspaper article.	**Verbs:** wore, built, ate, drank, grew, made **Food:** maize, cocoa, turkey, beans **Objects:** jewelry, pyramid **Phonics:** air, ear chair, fair, bear, wear	Think about others.
Checkpoint	Review Units 1–2	pp. 38–39	
Culture	Finland	pp. 40–41	
3 Up into space pp. 42–55	How can I design a vehicle for the future? • Describe space and the future. • Talk about the future using *will*. • Ask and answer about the future. • Write a brochure.	**Space words:** gravity, control panel, handle, fuel, lights, seat, radio, oxygen, screen, engine, Earth, planet **Phonics:** eer, ear near, hear, clear	Look after your world.
4 Dragons pp. 56–69	How can I invent a story about a fantasy animal? • Use words to describe dragons. • Talk about activities in the past. • Ask and answer about events in the past. • Write a witness statement.	**Story-telling words:** flew, swam, slept, burn, walk, dangerous, strong, brave, village, north, west, east **Phonics:** bl, pl, gl, cl, fl, sl blue, place, glass, clean, fly, sleep	Be the best you can.
Checkpoint	Review Units 3–4	pp. 70–71	
Culture	Panama	pp. 72–73	
5 Endangered animals pp. 74–87	How can I organize a campaign to save an animal? • Use animal and habitat words. • Use sentences with *if*. • Describe quantities with *more* and *fewer*. • Write a letter.	**Endangered animal words:** butterfly, wolf, otter, eagle, tiger, turtle, threat, habitat, pollution, chemicals, field, mountain **Phonics:** br, pr, fr, gr, cr, dr, tr brown, princess, frog, green, crab, dragon, tree	Care for wild animals.
6 Join in! pp. 88–101	How can I have a club fair? • Use club activity words. • Talk about rules using *should*. • Ask and answer using *should*. • Write a flyer.	**Hobby words:** meet, practice, get better, take part in, cheer, make new friends, neighborhood, contest, choir, chess, ice skating, drama **Phonics:** sc, sk, sm, sn, sp, st, sw skate, score, small, snail, space, start, sweet	Make new friends.
Checkpoint	Review Units 5–6	pp. 102–103	
Culture	Senegal	pp. 104–105	
7 Marvelous medicines pp. 106–119	How can I make a plant fact file? • Use illness and medicine words. • Explain why we do something. • Ask and answer about illnesses. • Write a doctor's report.	**Medical words:** patient, check up, medicine, neck, shoulder, stomachache, sore throat, bandage, cream, pill, temperature, thermometer **Phonics:** tw, qu twelve, twins queen, quick	Care for yourself.
8 Theme parks pp. 120–133	How can I make a model theme park ride? • Use theme park words. • Compare the past, present, and future. • Express my feelings. • Fill in a lost property form.	**Theme park words:** roller coaster, bumper cars, Ferris wheel, stand in line, take your seat, scream **Food:** popcorn, cotton candy, hotdogs, potato chips **Feelings:** scared, excited, interested, worried **Phonics:** j, g, c jelly, giant, ice	Be responsible.
Checkpoint	Review Units 7–8	pp. 134–135	
Culture	The United Kingom	pp. 136–137	

Writing	Structures		STEAM	Project and Review
	Language Lab Where are you from? I'm from Ecuador. Where is your aunt from? She's from Ecuador.	When's your birthday? It's on March 31st. When is your uncle's birthday?		
Write an SOS message.	**Language Lab** Dan is going to make a camp. Are you going to use a rope? Yes, I am. / No, I'm not.	**Communication** When are you going to go sailing? On Monday.	**Engineering:** Strong bridges **Experiment:** How can I build a bridge?	Plan a class adventure
News articles.	**Language Lab** The players kick the ball. The players kicked the ball. The players wore protection.	**Communication** When could you swim? I could swim when I was six. I could ride a bike two years ago.	**Math:** Number systems **Project:** Can you make a number square?	Make a model of an Aztec city
Brochures.	**Language Lab** We will live on a space colony. We won't need fuel. Will we recycle our waste?	**Communication** Where will you live? What will you eat? When will you arrive?	**Science:** Sound and communication **Experiment:** Can you make a telephone?	Design a vehicle for the future
Write a witness statement.	**Language Lab** The dragon was flying. They weren't eating. Was the dragon swimming? Yes, it was. / No, it wasn't.	**Communication** What were you doing when the fire started? I was swimming in the pool, when the fire started. I wasn't eating when the fire started.	**Science:** Flying machines **Experiment:** What model of airplane flies best?	Invent and tell a story about a fantasy animal
Letters	**Language Lab** If they build a lot more houses, it will be very noisy. If they don't care for the wildlife, it won't be a beautiful place.	**Communication** Are there more wolves than eagles? There are fewer bears than wolves. There are more owls than otters.	**Art and Design:** Light boxes **Experiment:** Can you make an animal light box?	Organize a campaign to save an animal
Flyers.	**Language Lab** You should tidy the space. You shouldn't push your friends.	**Communication** Should I clean the equipment? Yes!	**Science:** Sports and the senses **Experiment:** What senses do I need for balancing?	Have a club fair
Write a doctor's report.	**Language Lab** Doctors use medicine to make us better. Dentists use X-rays to see our teeth. Nurses use a thermometer to take our temperature.	**Communication** My head hurts. Does your ear hurt? Her stomach doesn't hurt.	**Science:** Tracking germs **Experiment:** How do you track germs?	Make a plant fact file
Fill in a form.	**Language Lab** She went to the dinosaur race. She is looking at the fossil exhibition. She will go on the roller coaster.	**Communication** I'm scared of roller coasters. I'm interested in dinosaurs. I'm worried about the long line for the Ferris wheel.	**Science:** Forces of motion **Project:** How can I test friction on a slide?	Make a model theme park ride

Welcome back!

How can I talk about myself?

Class 4A - Summer postcards
The children in Class 4A had a special task for the summer. All the children in the class wrote a postcard to a friend. On the first day of school, they showed the postcards in class.

1 Listen and number. Sing the song.

SONG TIME

How was your vacation?

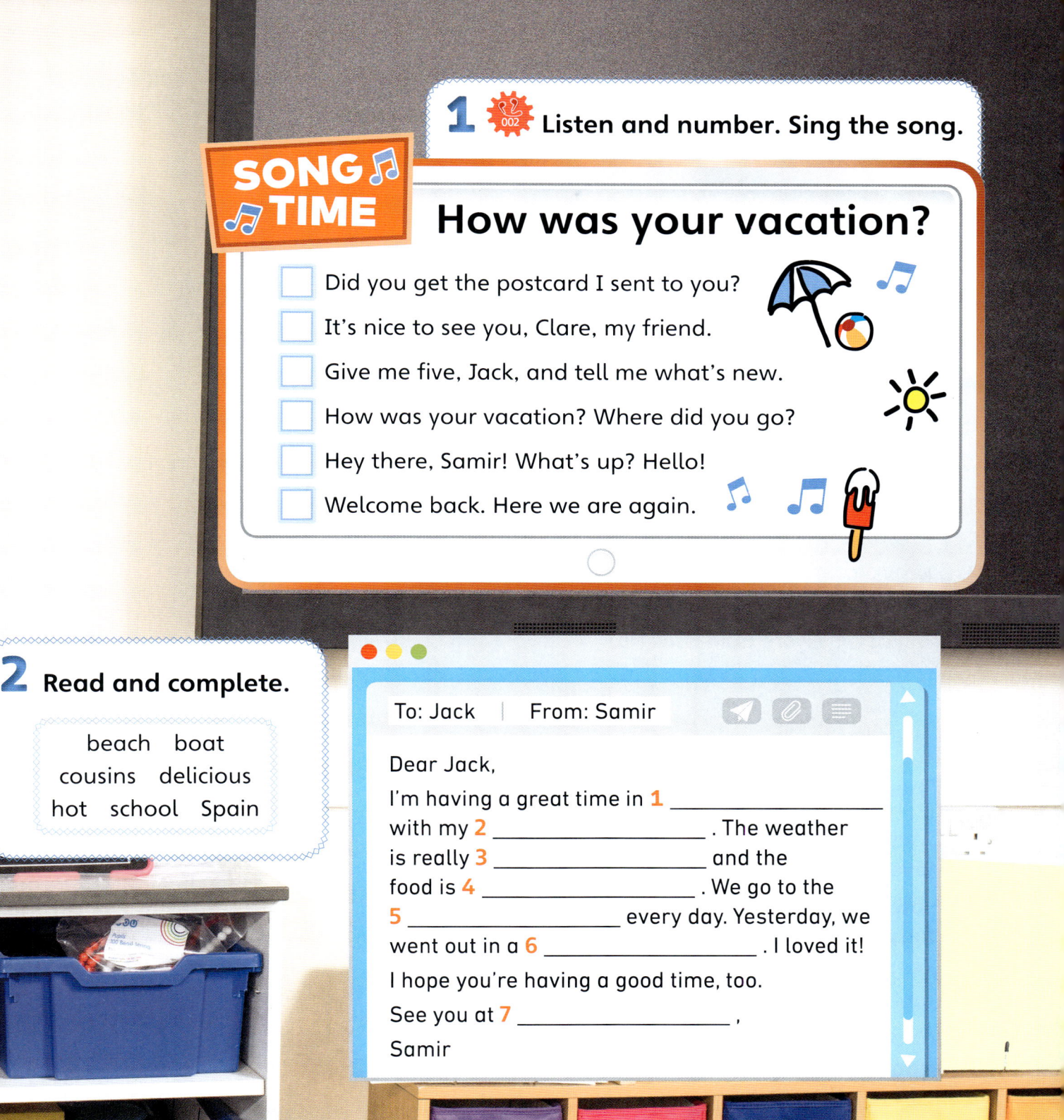

- [ ] Did you get the postcard I sent to you?
- [ ] It's nice to see you, Clare, my friend.
- [ ] Give me five, Jack, and tell me what's new.
- [ ] How was your vacation? Where did you go?
- [ ] Hey there, Samir! What's up? Hello!
- [ ] Welcome back. Here we are again.

2 Read and complete.

beach   boat
cousins   delicious
hot   school   Spain

To: Jack | From: Samir

Dear Jack,
I'm having a great time in **1** _____ with my **2** _____ . The weather is really **3** _____ and the food is **4** _____ . We go to the **5** _____ every day. Yesterday, we went out in a **6** _____ . I loved it!
I hope you're having a good time, too.
See you at **7** _____ ,
Samir

3 Was your vacation the same or different? Discuss with a partner.

I went to the beach, but I didn't go to Spain.

4 Imagine you are on vacation. Make a postcard for a friend.

five

Big families
VOCABULARY

I will learn family words.

1 Read and underline the countries.

Four generations of my family live in this town, but my family comes from all over the world!

The first generation were my grandparents. My dad's parents are from Russia and my mom's parents are from Ecuador.

The second generation here are my parents and my uncle. My mom and her sister are from the USA, and my dad and his brother are from Scotland.

My cousin, sister, and I are the third generation in the town. I live with my sister, my parents, and my grandpa.

Aunt Mary lives in Spain with her family, but Uncle John and his family live here.

My cousin Sally has a new baby! Eddie is the fourth generation of the family in this town!

2 Complete the family tree. Then answer the questions.

Aunt   Grandparents (2)   Parents   Uncle

1 Does Samir's mom have a sister? _____
2 How many aunts does Samir have? _____
3 Who are Edu and Bob's parents? _____
4 Who are Eddie's grandparents? _____

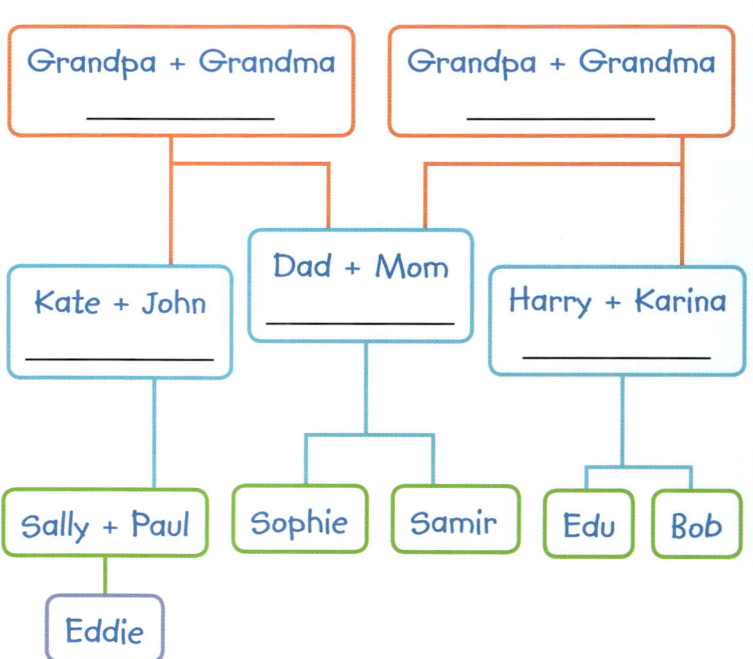

3 Ask and answer about Samir's family.

Who are Eddie's parents?

Language lab
GRAMMAR: WHEN ...?

I will learn to ask and answer about dates.

1 🎧 003 **Listen and check** ✓.

> When's your birthday? It's on October 3rd.

1 Who is having a party?
   a Samir's sister ☐   b Samir ☐   c Samir's best friend ☐

2 When is the birthday?
   a October 3rd ☐   b October 11th ☐   c October 28th ☐

3 When's the party?
   a October 3rd ☐   b October 5th ☐   c October 28th ☐

4 Where is the party?
   a in the park ☐   b at school ☐   c at home ☐

2 Read and write the the first letter of their names.

October

Mon	Tues	Weds	Thurs	Fri	Sat	Sun
	1st	2nd	3rd	4th	5th	6th
7th	8th	9th	10th	11th	12th ___	13th
14th	15th ___	16th	17th	18th	19th	20th ___
21st	22nd	23rd	24th	25th	26th	27th
28th	29th	30th	31st ___			

1 Lucy's birthday is on the fifteenth.
2 Harry's birthday is on the twentieth.
3 John's birthday is on the thirty-first.
4 Clare's birthday is on the twelfth.

3 💬 Make a bar chart showing your friends' birthdays.

"When is your birthday?"

4 Complete.

1 When's your friend _____'s birthday? It's on _____ .

2 _____'s your friend _____'s birthday? It's on _____ .

Story lab
READING

I will read a story about a birthday.

1 Look at the pictures. How old is Grandpa?

2 Read and listen.

The birthday party

1 Grandpa's birthday is at the end of February.

Let's have a party for Grandpa's 70th birthday!

70!

"That's a nice idea," Mom said. But Grandpa didn't want a party. "Don't worry about me," he said. "It's not an important day."

2 The children didn't agree. "Please can we have a party for Grandpa?" Sofia asked her Mom. "His 70th birthday is important!" "We can invite all the family" Samir said. "All right," Mom said.

Samir and Sofia talked to their cousins. "Can you come to Grandpa's party?"

The children did lots of work for the party, but Grandpa wasn't happy.

Remember! It's not a special birthday!

OK! OK!

Values Listen to others and say how you feel.

3 Answer the questions.

1. Why does the family want to celebrate Grandpa's birthday? _____
2. What did Grandpa say about the party at the start of the story? _____
3. Why did he say this? _____
4. Why wasn't Grandpa happy? _____
5. What is special about Grandpa's birthday? _____

3 The day before the party, Dad made a big birthday cake.

On the day of the party, Samir and Sofia went to the park. First, Samir's school friends arrived. They put lanterns and a piñata in the trees. Then the cousins arrived with their parents. Soon, everyone was there.

4 Finally, Grandpa and Mom arrived at the party. "Happy birthday," everyone shouted.

Everyone looked confused. "I was born on February 29th," Grandpa explained. "I have a birthday once every four years ... I'm not 70. I'm only 17!"

4 Read and complete.

> first   second   third   fourth   fifth   sixth   seventh

1. Dad was the _____ person to arrive at the party.
2. Uncle Karim was the _____ person to arrive at the party.
3. Samir and Sofia were the _____ and _____ people to arrive at the party.
4. Aunt Mary was the _____ person to arrive at the party.
5. The cousins were the _____ and _____ people to arrive at the party.

Arrival Times
Samir and Sofia: 4:00
Aunt Mary: 4:10
2 cousins: 4:30
Uncle Karim: 4:35
Dad: 4:50

5  Write an invitation for a party.

When you write an invitation, make sure you include who or what the party is for, where it is, and when it is.

6  Act out the story in groups.

1 Into the wild

How can we plan a class adventure?

1. Where are the children? What are they doing?

2 What are the children doing? Read and underline.

Playing outdoors is great! I really like climbing, swinging, collecting grass and leaves and making a camp. I like balancing on branches, swimming, and exploring. There are lots of great things to do outdoors!

3 What other activities can the children do? Discuss with a partner.

balance   climb   collect
make a camp   swing

branches   grass
leaves   rocks   trees

They can climb the trees.

They can't swing on the rocks.

4 Do an outdoor activities survey.

CODE CRACKER

1. Write four outdoor activities.
2. Write your name and check your two favorite activities.
3. Ask three friends and check their two favorite activities.
4. Add up the number of checks for each activity.

Activities				
Name: _____				
Name: _____				
Name: _____				
Name: _____				
Total ✓ checks				

What are your two favorite outdoor activities?

I like climbing trees and exploring.

In the forest
VOCABULARY

I will learn outdoor activity words.

1 🎧 **Listen and match. Sing the song.**

🎵 Adventure camp

We have a **wheel** and a **rope**.

We have **gloves** and **boots**.

We have **grass** and **matches**.

I said clap, clap, clap!
Clap, clap, clap!
I said stamp, stamp, stamp!
Stamp, stamp, stamp!
I said let's get ready for adventure camp.

We have a **whistle** and a **blanket**.

We have a **compass** and a **map**.

We have **branches** and **leaves**.

2 💡 **Look at 1. What are the items useful for? Think of one more item.**

climbing   cooking   crossing the stream
exploring   making a camp   swinging

The boots are useful for crossing the stream.

3 Look at **1**. Choose three items and make a list. Add your new item.

My list

4 🟣 Play *Get your equipment!*

- ⚀ climbing
- ⚁ cooking
- ⚂ crossing the stream
- ⚃ exploring
- ⚄ making a camp
- ⚅ swinging

1. Take turns to roll the dice.
2. Do you have the equipment for the activity?
3. Check all the equipment on your list and you're a winner!

My list

rope   map   compass   spoon

I rolled a one, that's "climbing"! I have a rope and that's useful for climbing.

5 🟢 Make your own picture dictionary. Draw and write in order from the least to most useful for playing outdoors.

 compass

 whistle

6 Ph 🔴006 ▶️ Listen and circle the correct tree. Then say.

A little girl with a skirt and a shirt heard a bird in a fir tree in the forest. Where's the fir tree with the bird the little girl heard?

7 Ph ▶️ Look at **6**. Find and circle words with the same sound as **learn**.

thirteen 13

Language lab
GRAMMAR: GOING TO ...

I will learn to talk about future plans using going to.

1 Watch the video.

Dan is **going to** make a camp.
He isn't **going to** use branches.
Clare and Pearl are **going to** use branches.
They aren't **going to** use leaves.
Are you **going to** ...? Yes, I am. / No, I'm not.

2 Listen and match.

- Clare
- Dan
- Fred
- Pearl

3 Look at **2**. Read and answer.

1 This child is going to use a wheel and rope. This child isn't going to use leaves or rocks. Who is it? _____

2 This child is going to use branches, rope, and an old door. This child isn't going to use rocks or a wheel. Who is it? _____

3 This child is going to use rocks and branches. This child isn't going to use a blanket or grass. Who is it? _____

4 This child is going to use leaves and grass. This child isn't going to use rope or boots. Who is it? _____

4 Look at 2. Play *Guess the picture*.

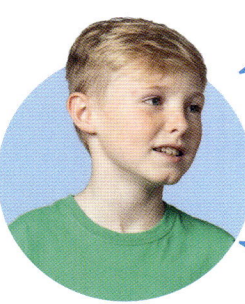

Are you going to use a rope?

Are you going to make a swing?

Are you going to make a treehouse?

Yes, I am.

No, I'm not.

Yes, I am.

5 What does it say? Use the spy's code to find out.

CODE CRACKER

THE SPY'S CODE

9 1 4 9 6 1 14

1 Mr. Red	2 the river	3 a black coat	4 the treehouse
5 Mr. Gray	6 boots	7 a compass	8 a rope
9 Madam Black	10 gloves	11 the bridge	12 a hat
13 a map	14 a whistle	15 the camp	16 a blanket

1 _____ and _____ are going to meet at _____ .

2 _____ is going to wear _____ .

3 _____ is going to take _____ .

6 Write a message with the spy's code.

_____
_____
_____

Story lab
READING

I will read a story about an island adventure.

1 Look at the pictures. What happens?

2 🎧 Read and listen.

Shipwrecked!

1 Jack and Alice were in their boat. Suddenly, there was a big storm. The waves threw the little boat up and down.

"We're going to crash! Quick! Jump out!"

2 Jack swam to the beach and looked around but Alice wasn't there. He blew his whistle three times and waited. Then he saw something far away. It was Alice!

"We don't have a sailboat now. What are we going to do?"

"Let's make an SOS message."

3 They collected rocks and wrote *SOS* on the sand. Then they waited for help. By the afternoon they were hungry and needed water. "Look! There are some trees up there. There has to be water," said Alice.

3 Complete the story path.

beach   trees
lighthouse
police station
river   sailboat

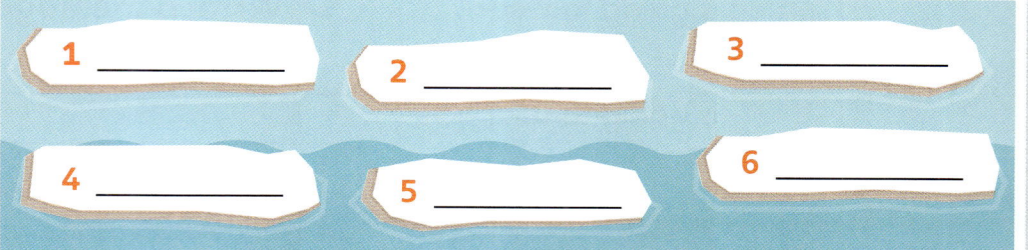

1 _____   2 _____   3 _____
4 _____   5 _____   6 _____

16 sixteen

4 They used their rope to climb up the rocks. On the other side, they found a river and some fruit trees.

Jack climbed up a tree. "Pass me the knife!" he shouted, and he cut some fruit. Then they filled their water bottles with water from the river. Alice took out her compass.

5 They walked for a long time. Then they saw a light. It was flashing on and off.

"That's the lighthouse. Come on!"

6 Officer Bond was happy to see the children. "The search party found your SOS message at Pirate Bay. How did you get here?" she asked.

That's north, so the river is flowing east.

Let's follow it.

Oh, it was easy! First, we …

Values Work together.

4 How did the children work together to find help? Discuss with a partner.

5 Write a story about Jack and Alice getting lost in a forest.

6 Act out the story in groups.

seventeen 17

Experiment lab
ENGINEERING: STRONG BRIDGES

I will learn how to build a bridge.

1 **Read, listen, and complete.**

deck

There are many different types of bridges, but they all have a road or pathway. Engineers call this the deck of the bridge. We can describe bridges by the position of the deck.

An arch bridge has a strong arch under the deck.
A truss bridge has a deck at the bottom of the structure.
A suspension bridge has a deck that hangs from cables.

1 _____ bridge   2 _____ bridge

3 _____ bridge

2 **Read, listen, and complete.**

pull up   push down

Imagine a heavy truck is going over a bridge. The weight of the truck is pushing down on the deck. The bridge isn't going to break. The structure of the bridge is pulling the deck in the opposite direction.

All bridges need a balance between a force pushing down and a force pulling up. A bridge breaks if one of the forces is greater than the other.

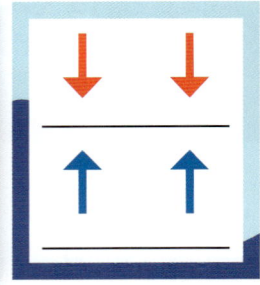

3 **Read and listen. Which photo has the most triangles?**

A triangle is a strong shape. Imagine you are pushing down on the point of a triangle. It's difficult to break. Triangles are used in many bridges to make the structure stronger.

4  Which bridge do you think is the strongest? Why?

5 How many triangles can you see in the pentagon?

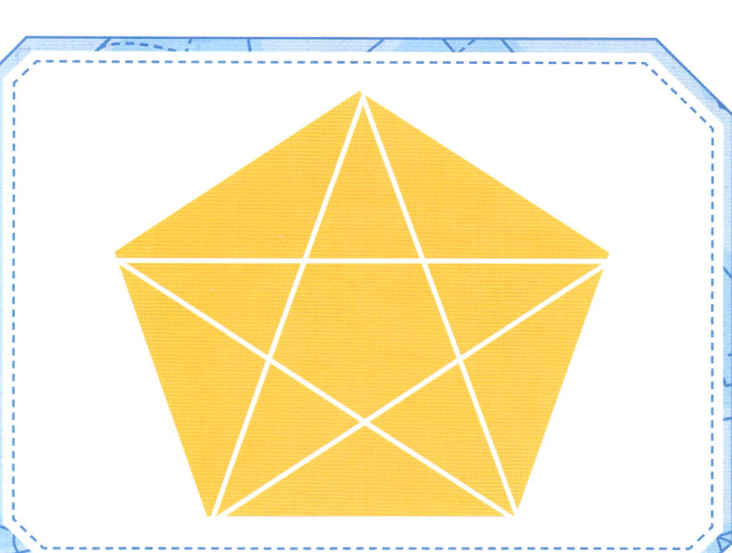

MATH ZONE Clue: Number the single shape triangles from 1 to 10. Then count the triangles with two, three, and five shapes.

EXPERIMENT TIME

How can I build a bridge?

Watch a video about a bridge.

1. Connect the popsicle sticks with clay to make triangles.
2. Connect the triangles to make a bridge.
3. Use the ruler for the deck of the bridge.
4. Test the strength of your structure with coins.

Materials
popsicle sticks   clay
a ruler   coins

There are ___ triangles in my bridge. It can carry ___ coins.

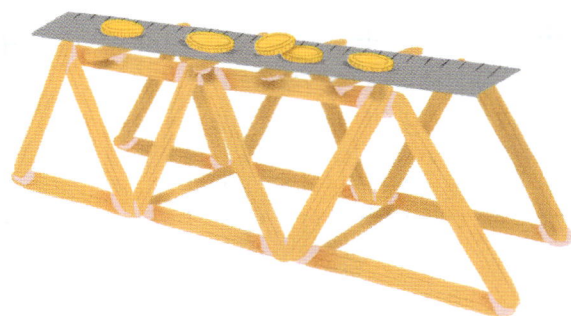

nineteen 19

Time phrases
COMMUNICATION

I will ask and answer about future plans.

1 🎧 012 **Listen and match.**

A time – **at** two o'clock
A day of the week – **on** Monday
A month of the year – **in** September
An amount of time – **for** two days

1. When are you going to go sailing again?
2. When are you going to see your parents?
3. How long are you going to stay here?
4. When are you going to visit Pirate Bay again?
5. When are you going to start school?

a. In September.
b. For two days.
c. On Monday.
d. At two o'clock.
e. Tomorrow.

2 💬 **Ask and answer about your next vacation with a partner.**

1. Press out the cards.
2. Write your name and your partner's name.
3. Complete the information for you.
4. Ask your partner and complete their information.

When are you going on your next vacation?

I'm going in March.

3 💬 **Play *Snap*!**

Harry is going on an adventure vacation in September.

Snap!

Writing lab
AN SOS MESSAGE

I will learn to write an SOS message.

Alice and Jack wrote an SOS message, put it in a bottle, and threw it into the sea.

1 Read and complete.   beach   food   forest   hungry   Pirate Bay   rocks   water

☐ May 3rd
☐ Dear Friend,
Our sailboat smashed on some _____ yesterday.
☐ There is a _____ behind the _____ .
☐ We are OK, but we are _____ and thirsty.
☐ We are going to stay here for four hours and then we are going to look for _____ and _____ .
☐ Please send help.
☐ From, Alice and Jack Samson
☐ (somewhere near _____)

2 Number the features in 1.

- ① = Who the letter is from
- ② = Who the letter is for
- ③ = Location
- ④ = Request for help
- ⑤ = Date
- ⑥ = Landscape
- ⑦ = Conditions
- ⑧ = Plans

3 Check ✓ a place and write an SOS message.

1 Write your message.
2 Don't forget to ask for help!
3 Put your message in a bottle.
4 Play *Pass the bottle*.

twenty-one 21

PROJECT AND REVIEW

Plan a class adventure.

Step 1

Research

Find out about local outdoor spaces.

- ☐ Make a list of different places near you.
- ☐ What activities can you do at each place?
- ☐ What equipment is going to be useful for the activities?

Places:
forest, beach, park

Step 2

Plan

Write a schedule for your adventure.

- ☐ Choose a place and a date for the outing.
- ☐ Decide the start and end times.
- ☐ Plan activities for the morning and the afternoon.
- ☐ Make a list of equipment.

Let's go to the river.

Yes! We can go in April.

OK. We are going to go to the river in April.

Let's go at 9 o'clock in the morning!

	Activities	Equipment
Morning	making a camp climbing	a blanket a rope
Afternoon	exploring swimming	a compass a towel

22 twenty-two

Step 3
Create

Make a plan for your adventure.

- [ ] Think of a name for your adventure.
- [ ] Find photos or draw pictures of the place.
- [ ] Include the date, the bus times, the schedule of activities, and the equipment.

River Outing!
Date: April 27th
Bus leaves: 9:00 a.m.
Activities: swimming, climbing rocks
Please bring: water, food for lunch, rope, boots, bathing suit

Show your plan to your family. Describe your adventure.

Step 4
Show and tell

Hold a class competition for the favorite adventure.

- [ ] Describe your plan for a class adventure.
- [ ] Explain the exciting activities.
- [ ] Your friends can choose three adventures.
- [ ] Find the favorite adventure in the class.

What are you planning for the class adventure?

We're going to go to the river.

In the afternoon, we're going to swim.

Now I can ...

... use outdoor activity words.

... talk about future plans using *going to*.

... ask and answer about future plans.

... write an SOS message.

twenty-three 23

2 Into the past

How can I make a model of an Aztec city?

1 What can you see in the museum?

2 Listen and complete.

AZTEC EXHIBITION

The photo shows the _____ of Tenochtitlan in the _____ century. The city was on an _____ in the middle of a _____. It was the capital city of the _____ Empire.

The Aztecs built pyramids. They made beautiful jewelry. They invented a calendar and they used pictograms for words.

3 💡 What do you think the pictograms mean? Look and complete.

dog   eagle   house   knife   rain   wind

4 ⚙️ Choose a word from 3. Create your own pictograms.

Amazing Aztecs
VOCABULARY

I will learn words to describe life in the past.

1 🎧 **Listen and number. Sing the song.**

SONG TIME

Long ago

The amazing Aztecs lived long ago.
Let's sing a song about long ago.

The amazing Aztecs looked up at the sky.
They **built** cities with **pyramids** that were high.
The amazing Aztecs **ate** fish and **turkey**.
They **drank cocoa** and they **made** gold **jewelry**.
The amazing Aztecs **grew maize** and **beans**.
They **wore** tunics and sandals. They didn't wear jeans.

(Repeat Chorus)

2 💡 **What did the Aztecs …? Discuss with a partner.**

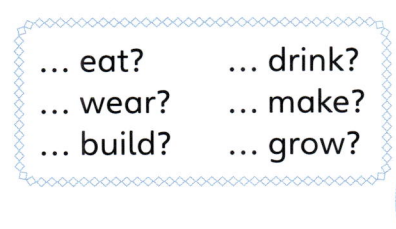

… eat?   … drink?
… wear? … make?
… build? … grow?

I think …

… they didn't build space stations.

… they wore jewelry.

26 twenty-six

3 Look at **1** and use the words to complete. Discuss your answers with a partner.

ate   drank   drink   eat   grew   grow   wear   wore

Atzi lived in a big house in the city.
She _____ . She didn't _____ .
She _____ . She didn't _____ .
She _____ . She didn't _____ .

Zuma worked in the fields outside the city.
He _____ . He didn't _____ .
He _____ . He didn't _____ .
He _____ . He didn't _____ .

4 Make your own picture dictionary. Draw and label the new words in two groups: *Actions* and *Objects*.

Actions – built

Objects – pyramid

5 Listen and check. Then say.

a

b

There's a fair in the square with a bear on a chair. And the bear wears a feather in its hair.

6 Say it again as quickly as you can.

twenty-seven 27

Language lab
GRAMMAR: PAST AND PRESENT

> I will learn to compare the past and the present.

1  **Watch the video.**

The players **kick** the ball.
The players **kicked** the ball.

The ancient Mayans and Aztecs

The ancient Mayans lived in southern Mexico and Central America about 4,000 years ago. The ancient Aztecs lived in northern Mexico about 700 years ago.

Did you know that Mayans and Aztecs still live in Mexico and Central America today?

2 Look, read, and match.

1 We play the game on a field. It is 109 meters long with a net at each end. The ball weighs about 450 grams. There are two teams. They kick or head the ball. They don't touch the ball with their hands. The players wear protection on their legs and goalkeepers wear gloves. The aim is to get the ball into the opposite goal.

2 They played the game on a court. It was 50 meters long with a ring at each side. The ball weighed about 4 kilograms. There were two teams. They hit the ball with their elbows, knees, hips, and head. They didn't touch the ball with their hands. The players wore protection on their faces, hips, and legs. The aim was to get the ball through the rings.

3 **Look at 2. What is the same and different? Discuss with a partner.**

> Players wore protection on their heads for the ball game.

> Players wear protection on their legs for soccer.

28 twenty-eight

4 Number the sentences in order.

CODE CRACKER

① ② ③ ④ ⑤ ⑥ Score a goal

- ☐ She kicks the ball towards the goal.
- ☐ The player puts the ball on the penalty spot.
- ☐ She runs towards the ball.
- ☐ She steps back.
- ☐ She waits for the whistle.

5 Read and complete.

bowling/totoloque   don't kick/didn't kick   play/played
stand/stood   throw/threw   use/used   wear/wore

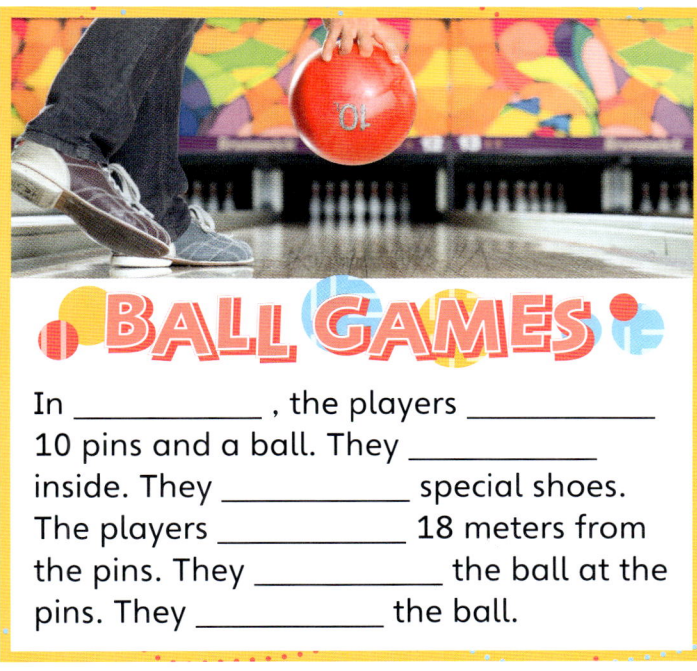

BALL GAMES

In _____ , the players _____ 10 pins and a ball. They _____ inside. They _____ special shoes. The players _____ 18 meters from the pins. They _____ the ball at the pins. They _____ the ball.

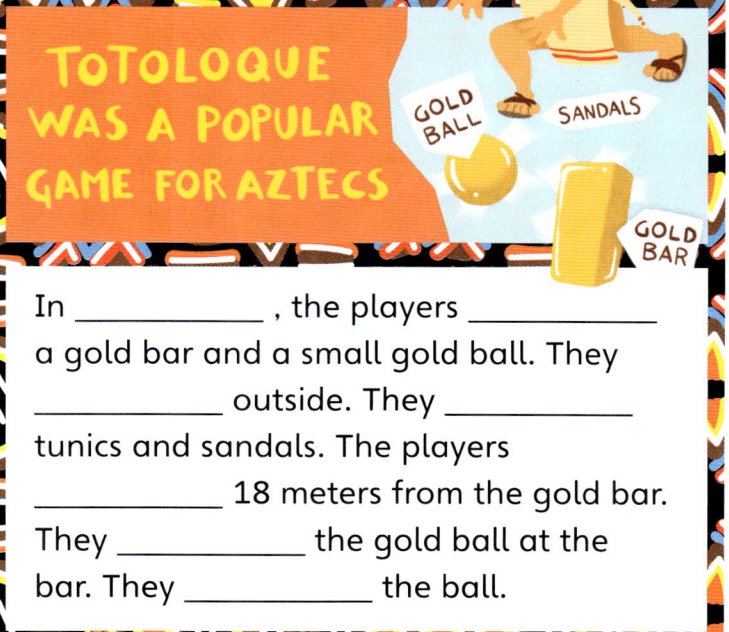

In _____ , the players _____ a gold bar and a small gold ball. They _____ outside. They _____ tunics and sandals. The players _____ 18 meters from the gold bar. They _____ the gold ball at the bar. They _____ the ball.

6  Play *Mime the game*.

Story lab
READING

I will read a story about a lost treasure.

1 Look at the pictures. Is the story set in the past, present, or future?

2 Read and listen.

THE BLACK STONE

1 Jacobo liked digging in his backyard. Sometimes he found old pieces of pottery and metal in the earth.

"Many years ago, this town was a large city," Jacobo's father explained. "There was a pyramid and a great treasure. Many people looked for the treasure, but nobody found it."

One day, Jacobo's spade hit a piece of black stone. Jacobo picked it up and cleaned it. It had a square shape at the top and a strange design. It looked very old, but the design was familiar.

2 Jacobo showed the stone to his parents. "What did people use this for?" he asked.

"Maybe women wore it in their hair," his mother said.
"Maybe people ate with it," his father said.

Values Think about others.

3 Who does the treasure belong to? Discuss with a partner.

1. It belongs to Jacobo and Angie.
2. It belongs to the city.
3. It belongs to Jacobo's parents.

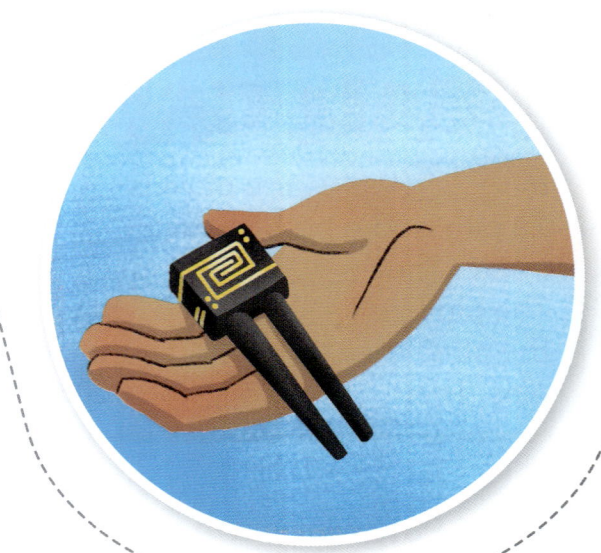

3 The next day, Jacobo showed the stone to his friend, Angie. "I saw that design this morning," she said. Angie lived near the ruins of the old city. Grass covered most of the ruins, but there were some walls from the ancient buildings.

Jacobo looked up. "There it is again!" he said. "And again." They followed the designs to a small hill. "I can see something black under the grass," Jacobo said. The children pulled at the grass. There was a door.

In the middle of the door, there was a keyhole. Jacobo looked at the stone. It was the same shape. He put it into the keyhole and turned. Slowly the door opened. Inside the room, the children could see many gold boxes full of jewelry and coins. "It's the lost treasure!"

4 Read the story again and underline an important sentence …

… at the start of the story.   … in the middle of the story.   … at the end of the story.

5 Complete the story summary.

Title: _____
Setting: _____
People in the story: _____

At the start of the story, _____
_____

In the middle of the story, _____
_____

At the end of the story, _____
_____

6 Act out the story in groups.

thirty-one 31

Experiment lab
MATH: NUMBER SYSTEMS

I will learn how to make a number square.

1 **Read, listen, and complete.**   Egyptian   Chinese   Mayan

ANCIENT NUMBER SYSTEMS

Although there are different languages and alphabets all over the world, in most parts of the world we use the same number system. This system is called the Arabic number system and it uses a symbol for zero. In ancient times, there were many different number systems.

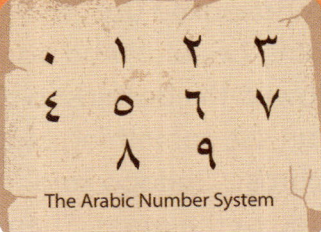
The Arabic Number System

The ancient _____ number system had dots and lines. The numbers from one to four were dots. Number five was a line. The numbers after that were dots and lines. The Mayans were the first people to have a symbol for zero.

The ancient _____ number system used pictures called hieroglyphs for numbers. Number one was a stick, ten was an arch, a hundred was a rope, a thousand was a flower, ten thousand was a finger, and a hundred thousand was a tadpole. The hieroglyph for a million was a man looking surprised!

The ancient _____ number system used vertical and horizontal lines. When they wrote a big number they used vertical lines for the units and horizontal lines for the tens. They wrote the numbers on a counting board. A blank square was a zero in the number.

2 Read and answer.

1. Which systems had a symbol for zero?
2. Which system used pictures to represent numbers?
3. Which system had a picture representing one million?
4. Which system do we use all over the world today? Why do you think people all over the world use this system?

3 Use the ancient number systems to write and answer the sum.

MATH ZONE

Daisy has five candies and Robert has twelve. How many candies do they have between them?
Which system do you think is the easiest? Why?

4 Read and answer.

CODE CRACKER

a	b	c	d	e	f	g	h	i	j	k	l	m
2	4	7	11	16	22	29	__	__	56	__	__	92

n	o	p	q	r	s	t	u	v	w	x	y	z
106	121	__	154	172	__	211	232	254	__	301	326	__

Look at the first numbers. What do we add to each number to make the next number?

5 Complete the number code. Then write your friend's name in code.

This is your name, Danny!

11, 2, 106, 106, 326

EXPERIMENT TIME

Can you make a number square?

Make the sum of three numbers in any row. What do you notice? Make a number square.

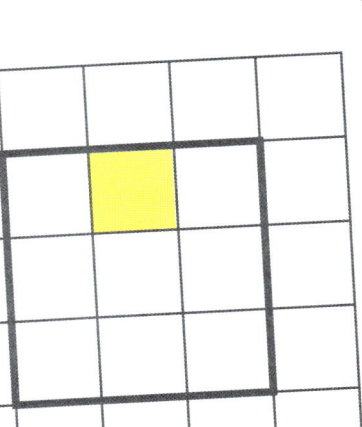

1. Write the first number for your sequence in the yellow square.
2. Now move up one square and right one square.
3. If this takes you out of the square, go down to the bottom box in the square and write the number.
4. Now repeat. Move up one square and to the right one square.
5. If this takes you out of the square, go to first left square in the same row.
6. Now repeat. Move up one square and to the right one square. If there is a number in the box already or if you are in a corner outside of the square, go down one square from where you started.
7. Now continue using the rules above.

thirty-three 33

Could and ago
COMMUNICATION

> I will ask and answer using **could** and **ago**.

1 🎧 Listen and check ✓ or cross ✗.

> When **could** you **read**?
> I **could read** when I was six.
> I **couldn't read** six years ago.

1
2
3
4
5
6
7
8

2 💬 Look at **1**. Ask and answer with a partner.

> When could you swim?
> I could swim when I was six.

3 Read and complete.

MATH ZONE

The year now is _____
Year I learned to swim: _____
Year I learned to ride a bike: _____
I could swim _____ years ago.
I could ride a bike _____ years ago.

4 💬 Choose an action from **1**. Do a survey and complete the table.

Action: _____

Name	How many years ago?

> When did you learn to read?
> When I was six. That's four years ago.

Writing lab
NEWS ARTICLES

I will learn to write a newspaper article.

1 Read the newspaper article and underline …

1. … a fact, i.e., something that happened.
2. … someone's opinion, i.e., what someone thinks.
3. … a quotation, i.e., what someone said.

☐ Children find lost treasure

☐ by Hugo Lopez   ☐ September 17th

Last Saturday, two local children made an amazing discovery. Jacobo, from San Andrés, found a key in his backyard. "At first I didn't know it was a key," Jacobo explained. Jacobo's friend, Angie saw the design on some walls near her house. Together, they found a hidden door and a room with treasure.

The children informed the local museum and now historians are studying the objects. The treasure probably belonged to the last ruler of the city. "We think it is more than 500 years old," the museum director said.

☐ Local heroes, Jacobo and Angie

2 Number the features in 1.

1. photo
2. headline
3. dateline
4. by line
5. photo caption

3 Check ✓ a lost treasure you find. Then ask and answer with a partner.

a map ☐   a painting ☐   a statue ☐   a coin ☐   a treasure chest ☐

- Where did you find it?
- When did you find it?
- What is it?
- How old is it?
- What did you do with it?

4 Write a newspaper article about your partner's treasure.

PROJECT AND REVIEW

Make a model of an Aztec city

Step 1

Research

Find out about Aztec cities and materials.

- [ ] Make a list of the buildings and places in an Aztec city.
- [ ] Find pictures of the buildings and places.
- [ ] In groups, discuss how to make the model.
- [ ] Make a list of materials you need.

Buildings:
pyramid, palace, …

Other places:
hill, lake, …

Materials:
clay, paint, boxes …

> We can make the palace from an old box.

> We can use clay for the pyramid.

Step 2

Plan

Make a street plan of the city.

- [ ] How many building are you going to make?
- [ ] Work in pairs and choose a type of building.
- [ ] As a class, plan the position of the buildings in the city.
- [ ] Make a street plan.

Type of place:	pyramid	houses
Number:	2	6
Names:	Juan, Elisa	David, Ana

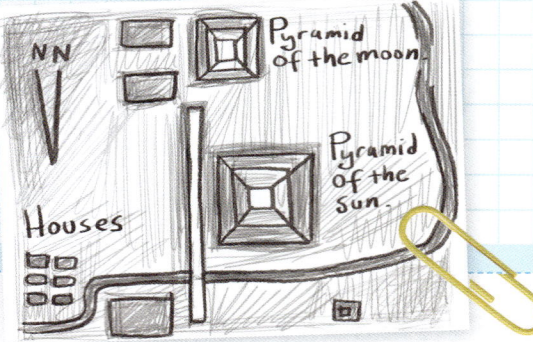

> The small houses were on the outskirts of the city.

36 thirty-six

Step 3

Create

▷ Make the city.

- ☐ Work with a partner and make your buildings.
- ☐ Follow the plan and place the buildings on a large board.
- ☐ Invent a name for the city and a date.

Let's call the city Tloto.

OK. I think the city was powerful 600 years ago.

Show your family a photo of the model. Explain how you made it.

Step 4

Show and tell

▷ Imagine daily life in the city.

- ☐ Work in groups.
- ☐ Imagine a family.
- ☐ Choose a house and invent their daily life.
- ☐ Compare their life to life now.

The family lived near the palace.

The father made jewelry.

Now I can ...

- ... use words to describe life in the past.
- ... compare the past and present.
- ... ask and answer using *could* and *ago*.
- ... write a newspaper article.

thirty-seven 37

1 Checkpoint
UNITS 1 AND 2

	5 years ago	wore	A going to make	not going to make
Z on the weekend		Z	on Saturday	
couldn't make	A going to use	Z swim / swims		A in March
Z 2 years ago	wear / wears	in the summer	A	don't / doesn't swim
A	don't / doesn't wear	Z every day		
	Z couldn't swim	not going to use	at 5 o'clock	didn't wear
	made	ate		play / plays

38 thirty-eight

1. 🎧 Listen and write G in the squares.

George

2. Read and check ✓ the true sentences.

Z = Zoe   A = Antonio

Zoe   Antonio

1. Antonio is going to make a camp in March.
2. He's going to use a blanket.
3. He's going to wear some sandals.
4. Zoe couldn't swim two years ago.
5. Now, she swims on the weekend.
6. She doesn't play in a camp.

3. Complete the squares on the board. Then write a sentence.

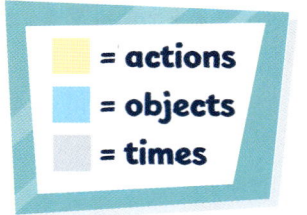

= actions
= objects
= times

George _____
_____ _____ .

4. Write about yourself.

I _____ _____ _____ .
I _____ _____ _____ .
I _____ _____ _____ .
I _____ _____ _____ .

5. 💬 Ask and answer with a partner.

Could you swim five years ago?
Yes, I could.

What are you going to do on the weekend?
I'm going to play with my friends.

What did you eat on Saturday?
I ate ice cream.

What do you wear in the summer?
I wear sandals and a hat.

thirty-nine 39

The Saami people
CULTURE

1 🎧 **Listen and check ✓ the true sentences.**

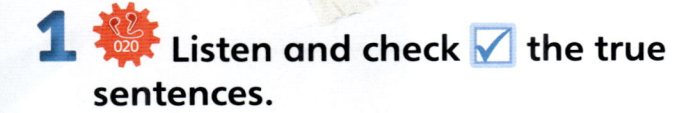

1. The homelands of the Saami people are in the North of Europe. ☐
2. In the winter, the Saami people followed reindeer to the north. ☐
3. The Saami people moved camp. ☐
4. The Saami people drank cow's milk. ☐
5. All of the Saami homelands are in Finland. ☐
6. In the 21st century, most Saami people live in tents. ☐
7. Reindeer herders use modern tools. ☐
8. The Saami people have their own language. ☐

2 **Look at 1. Correct the false sentences.**

_____
_____
_____

3 💬 **What is Hugo going to do in the summer? Compare and discuss with a partner.**

> I think he's going to sleep in a tent, but I'm going to sleep in my bed.

FINLAND

Finland is the eighth biggest country in Europe, but the population is only about 5.5 million people. Finland is close to the North Pole.

Fun Fact!

During summer there are some days in Finland when the sun shines all day and there is no night sky.

Hugo

My name is Hugo. My life is very different in the winter and the summer. Now it's winter, and I live in a town and I go to school. But in the summer, I'm going to follow the reindeer with my grandfather. The reindeer go north in the summer because it's warmer than in the winter. We often sleep outdoors in the wild.

4 Read and choose the missing sentences.

Duodji

Duodji are an important part of Saami traditions. The Saami made objects from the materials around them. ☐ Duodji were beautiful, but they were also useful and easy to carry. ☐

Nowadays, the Saami people still make duodji. Many of the objects are part of the Saami's traditional clothes. ☐ The traditional colors for Saami clothes are blue, red, yellow, and green. ☐

Duodji

1. These colors are also on the Saami flag.
2. The Saami made knives, containers, and bags.
3. They make boots, hats, and gloves in bright colors.
4. They used reindeer skin or fur from animals.

5. What do the colors and shapes on the flag mean? Discuss with a partner.

My Culture

6 Make a friendship bracelet.

Choose three of the traditional Saami colors.

You need a 10 cm strip of cloth or wool for each color.

What to do:
1. Tie the three pieces of wool or cloth together at one end.
2. Braid the pieces to make a bracelet.
3. Tie a knot at the other end and make a loop.

7 What do the colors mean? Discuss with a partner.

Blue is for the summer sky and green is for grass.

3 Up into space

How can I design a vehicle for the future?

1 Look and think of questions about the photo. Then ask and answer with a partner.

2 🎧 021 **Read the text. Then listen and answer.**

UP INTO SPACE

Welcome to the space center. In space, there is no gravity. This is called *zero gravity* and this is why astronauts float. In the space center, you can experience zero gravity. You will float! There are handles so you can move around and a control panel which shows you important information about the space station.

3 💬 **What can you do in zero gravity? Discuss with a partner.**

- exercise ☐
- take a shower ☐
- eat soup ☐
- get dressed ☐
- drink from an open cup ☐
- brush your teeth ☐

We think it's impossible to take a shower.

Why?

4 Complete the code.

CODE CRACKER

| 0 | 1 | 2 | 3 | 4 |
| 5 | 6 | 7 | 8 | 9 |

The code to enter the room is
7 ____ ____ ____ ____.

↑ → → ↓ ← ↑ ← ←

Lift off!
VOCABULARY

I will learn words to describe a control panel.

1 Listen and number. Sing the song.

Commander Sally Holms is the captain of the spacecraft. She is going to leave **Earth** on a mission to another **planet**. She is checking the percentages on the **control panel** before lift-off.

CONTROL PANEL

SCREEN — ENGINES — FUEL

SONG TIME

Commander Sally

Control panel on, check the **oxygen**.
Commander Sally, do you hear? Yes, I hear you loud and clear.
Computer on, check the **fuel**.
Commander Sally, do you hear? Yes, I hear you loud and clear.
Radio on, check the **lights**.
Commander Sally, do you hear? Yes, I hear you loud and clear.
Screen on, check the **gravity**.
Commander Sally, do you hear? Yes, I hear you loud and clear.
Take your **seat**. Hold the **handles** tight.
Fire all **engines**! Three, two, one!
Commander Sally, have a nice flight!

RADIO — OXYGEN — LIGHTS — COMPUTER — GRAVITY

Commander Sally, do you hear?

Yes, I hear you loud and clear!

2 What does Commander Sally need for …? Discuss with a partner.

breathing   communicating
controlling   moving   working

She needs the control panel for controlling the spacecraft.

44 forty-four

3 Match and color in the circles.

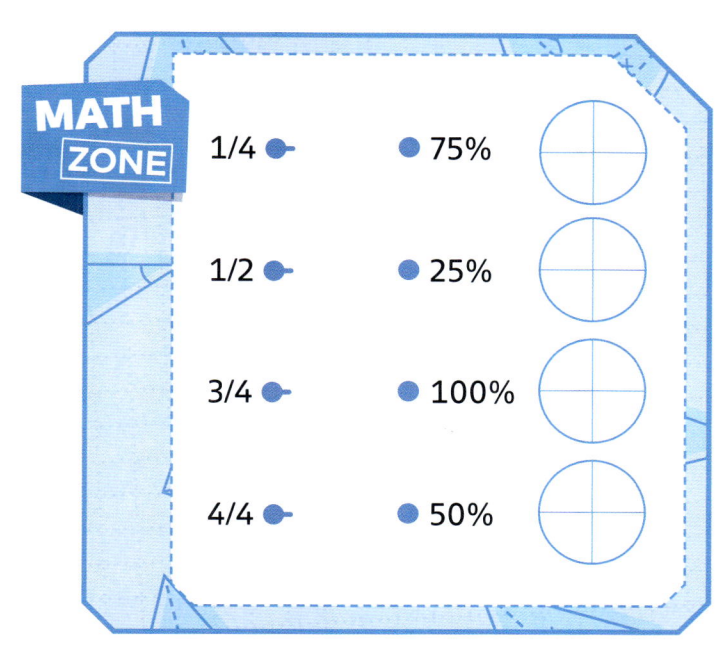

MATH ZONE

1/4 — 75%
1/2 — 25%
3/4 — 100%
4/4 — 50%

4 Color the levels. Then ask and answer with a partner.

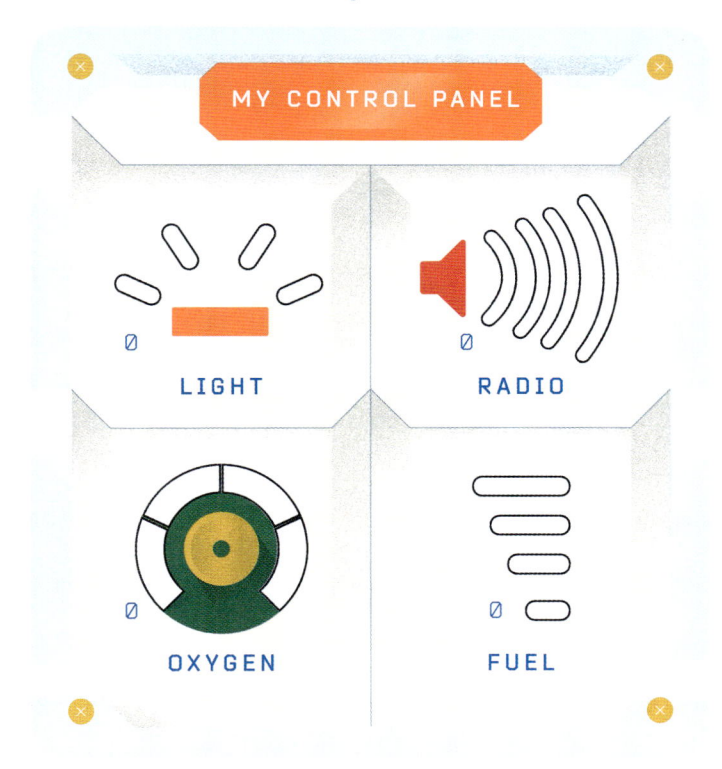

MY CONTROL PANEL

LIGHT   RADIO
OXYGEN   FUEL

What percentage is your fuel at?
It's at fifty percent.

5 Make your own picture dictionary of a control panel with a color-coded key.

● fuel
● oxygen
● radio

6 Listen and read. Check ✓ the answer.

Commander Sally hears loud and clear.
And off she goes for nearly a year.
The planet isn't far, it's really near.
So, where does she go?

☐ Mars
☐ Mercury
☐ Jupiter

7 Find and circle words with the same sound as **ear** in 6.

forty-five 45

Language lab
GRAMMAR: *WILL* AND *WON'T*

I will learn to talk about the future using will.

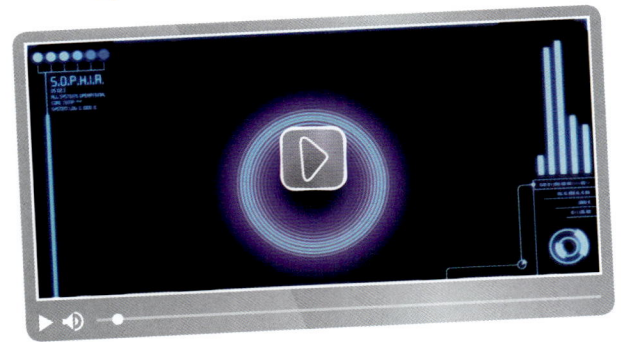

1 Watch the video.

We **will** live on a space colony.
We **won't** need fuel.
Will we recycle our waste?
Yes, we **will**.
No, we **won't**.

2 Read and number the pictures.

_____ floor
_____ floor
_____ floor
_____ floor
_____ floor
_____ floor

What do you think life will be like in the future?

I think in the future we will live in a space colony like this one. The colony will orbit Earth. We won't need fuel because we will get all our energy from the Sun. There will be six floors. We will grow food on the 6th floor because it will have the most sunlight. We will recycle all our waste on the 1st floor because it will be the darkest. We will live on the 3rd floor, but we won't live in houses. We will play on the 2nd floor and we will work on the 4th floor. We will do our shopping on the 5th floor.

3 Read and write four sentences. Discuss with a partner.

We will …
We won't …

- wear school uniforms.
- wear oxygen masks.
- use radios to talk to friends.
- have computer screens in our hands.
- have cars without engines.
- live on another planet.

We won't have cars without engines.

I don't agree.

Why?

Because we will have electric cars.

1 In the future, _____
2 _____
3 _____
4 _____

4 Complete the lists.

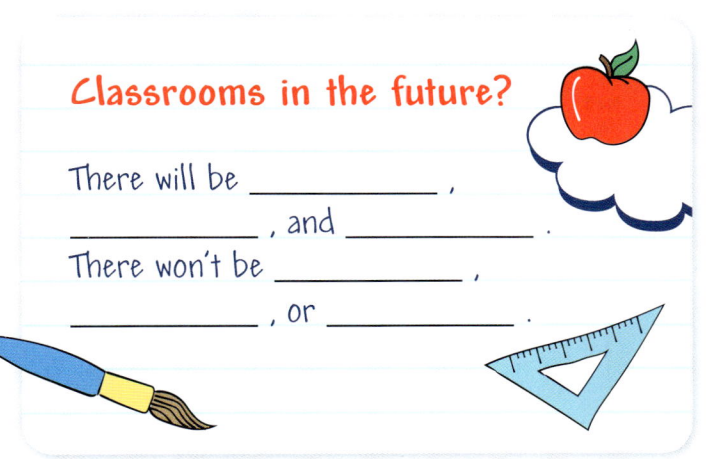

Classrooms in the future?

There will be _____, _____, and _____.
There won't be _____, _____, or _____.

Bedrooms in the future?

There will be _____, _____, and _____.
There won't be _____, _____, or _____.

5 Play *Find your words*.

Will there be beds in the bedroom?

No, there won't. Will there be screens in the classroom?

Yes, there will.

forty-seven 47

Story lab
READING

I will read a story about a space colony.

1 Look at the pictures. Where do you think they are?

2 Read and listen.

COLONY 369

1 Hundreds of years ago, Earth was very polluted. People went to live on space colonies. One day, there was a problem with the control panel on Colony 369.

Scientists worked day and night to find a solution, but nothing worked.

2 Nia wished humans could live on Earth again. Her robot friend, Bob, told her there were robots on Earth. Bob used his special radio to communicate with them.

CONTROL ROOM

We only have oxygen for two more years.

What is Earth like now?

Earth is perfect.

That's the solution! We will live on Earth.

No. We won't open the portal because humans will destroy the planet again.

Values Look after your world.

3 Imagine you are Nia and complete.

We promise ...

we will _____.
we won't _____.
Signature: _____

4 Why do the Earth robots trust the children? Discuss with a partner.

3 So Nia and Bob worked out a plan with the Earth robots. All the children went to a secret place. The Earth robots opened the special space door, but only for the children.

Wow! This is so beautiful!

And we can play outside!

4 Back on the colony, the adults were worried. Where were all the children? Then suddenly the screens came on.

Hello! This is Nia. We are on Earth. Will you promise that you won't pollute Earth ever again? Then we will open the space door.

5 That night the people from Colony 369 returned to the beautiful Earth.

This is the best solution. We promise we won't pollute the land, air, or water. Thank you, children!

5 Number the sentences in order. Which sentences happen before the story begins?

- [ ] The Earth robots open the special door.
- [ ] Nia and Bob find a solution.
- [ ] Colony 369 only has oxygen for two years.
- [ ] People polluted Earth.
- [ ] The adults promise they won't pollute Earth.
- [ ] People moved to a space colony.
- [ ] The children arrive on Earth.
- [ ] The adults arrive on Earth.

6 Act out the story in groups.

forty-nine 49

Experiment lab
SCIENCE: SOUND AND COMMUNICATION

I will learn how to make a telephone.

Sound is a type of energy that is made when things vibrate. For example, when we hear the engine of a car. We use sound to communicate with others over short and long distances.

1 Check ✓ the pictures that show sound being used.

2 Read, listen, and complete.

Sound travels in waves. Sound waves get quieter as they travel. That's why we hear sound louder when we are close to the source, and quieter when we are far away. Sound waves travel in all directions. They have to travel through something, like a gas, liquid, or solid that will vibrate, for example: air, water, or glass. They cannot travel in outer space because there isn't anything that will vibrate.

3 Read, listen, and draw the echo.

When sound waves hit hard objects, they change direction and we hear an echo of the sound. If you stand in an empty room and shout, you will hear the echo. When sound waves hit soft objects, the sound waves stop and we don't hear an echo. We use soft materials to make sound quieter. For example, in music rooms or near busy streets.

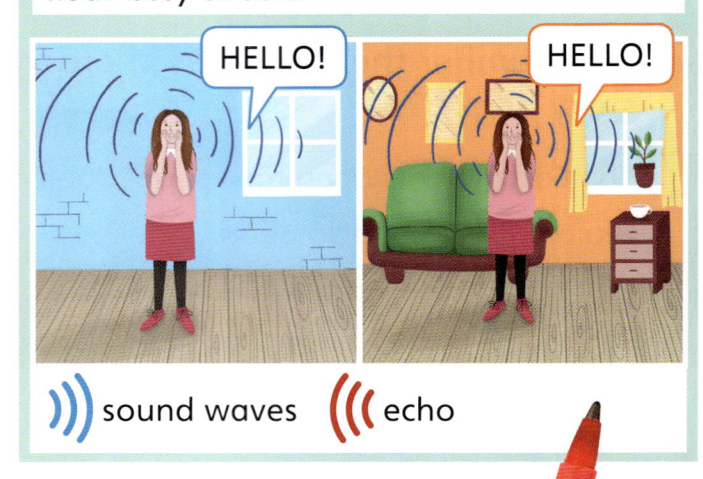

))) sound waves   (((echo

50 fifty

4 Read and look. Then spell a partner's name in Morse code.

Morse code is an old system for sending messages. It uses short and long sounds to spell words. Written Morse code uses dots for the short sounds and dashes for the long sounds.

Dot dot dot … dot dash … dash dash.

```
A ●—        H ●●●●      O ———        V ●●●—
B —●●●      I ●●        P ●——●       W ●——
C —●—●      J ●———      Q ——●—       X —●●—
D —●●       K —●—       R ●—●        Y —●——
E ●         L ●—●●      S ●●●        Z ——●●
F ●●—●      M ——        T —
G ——●       N —●        U ●●—
```

5 Listen and write the word. Then play Guess the word.

CODE CRACKER

The binary tree helps you learn Morse code. The left branches are dots and the right branches are dashes.

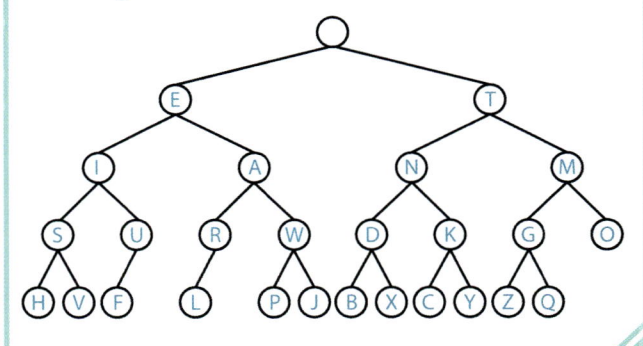

EXPERIMENT TIME

Can you make a telephone?

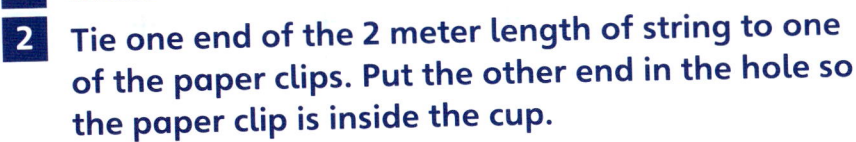

1. Make a hole in the bottom of each cup.
2. Tie one end of the 2 meter length of string to one of the paper clips. Put the other end in the hole so the paper clip is inside the cup.
3. Put the other end of the string in the hole in the other cup. Tie a paper clip on the end so that it is inside the other cup.
4. Give one cup to your friend and walk away until the string is tight. Talk normally into your cup and tell your friend to listen.
5. Test your telephone several times speaking louder and quieter each time.

Materials
- two plastic cups
- a 2 meter length of string
- 2 metal paper clips

1. What vibrates when you talk into the cup?

2. What do the sound waves travel along?

fifty-one 51

Questions with *will*
COMMUNICATION

*I will ask and answer about the future using **will**.*

1 🗨 **Ask and answer with a partner.**

> **Warning!** Earth is polluted. We will move to a space colony soon. Everybody will work together to plan for our future.

Where will you live?
What will you eat?
When will you arrive?
Who will you see?
How will you live?

- Who will the commander be?
- Who will the navigator be?
- Where will you go?
- When will you go?
- How will you get there?
- What fuel will you use?

2 ⚙ **Discuss the future with a partner.**

1. Press out the cards.
2. Complete the questions with *what*, *where*, *when*, *who*, and *how*.
3. Answer the questions for you.
4. Ask your partner and write their answers.

ON THE SPACE COLONY
1. _____ will you live?
2. _____ will you live with?
3. _____ will you eat?
4. _____ will you wear?
5. _____ will you get oxygen?
6. _____ will you get fuel?
7. _____ will you come back to Earth?
8. _____ will you travel back to Earth?

_____'s answers

3 🗨 **Explain your plans to your friends.**

> I will go to a space colony near Mars. I will live in a floating house.

> How will you get inside your house?

52 fifty-two

Writing lab
A BROCHURE

I will learn to write a brochure.

1 Read and number.

WELCOME TO PAIDON CITY
the city of the future!

A paragraph is a group of sentences about one main idea or topic.

1 = work places
2 = transportation
3 = schools
4 = outdoor places
5 = houses

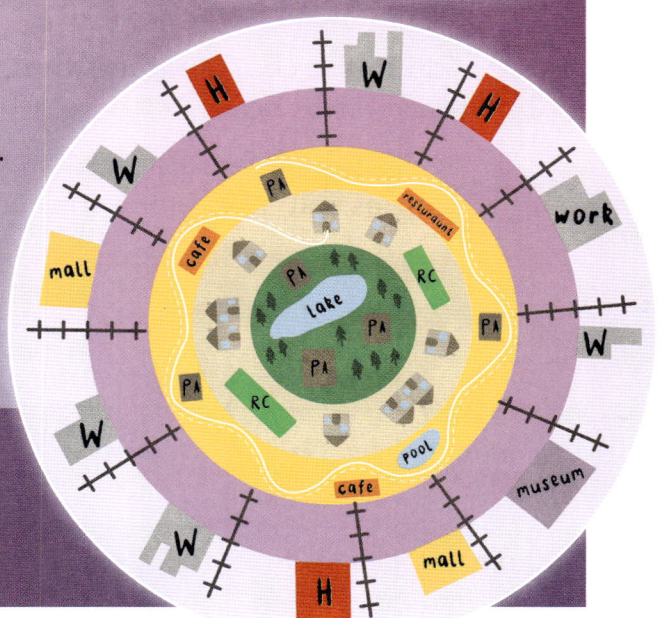

☐ In the center of the city there will be a school in a big forest. All the children will walk to school.

☐ The houses will be small but beautiful. The houses will have gardens and spaces to leave bicycles.

☐ The park will have swimming pools, outdoor sports centers, and a special zero-gravity play area in the park.

☐ There won't be any traffic, noise, or pollution in Paidon City. People will take electric trains to work.

☐ There will be clean buildings for people to work in. Nearby, there will be shopping malls and hospitals.

Will you come and live in **Paidon City**?

Call **836-555-1116** to plan a visit.

2 Look at **1**. How do we know it will be a healthy city? Underline the answers.

3 Imagine you are making a space city and complete.

Name of the city: _____
Outdoor places: _____   Transportation: _____
Work places: _____   Schools: _____
Houses: _____   Other places: _____

4 Make a brochure for your space city.

fifty-three 53

PROJECT AND REVIEW

Design a vehicle for the future

Step 1

Research

> Find out about vehicles.

- ☐ Make a chart with how vehicles move.
- ☐ Add to the chart features that the vehicles have.
- ☐ Decide which features the vehicles will have in the future.

	Now	In the future
land	cars have wheels	no wheels
air	planes have wings	different types of wings
water	sailboats have sails	they will have balloons

Step 2

Plan

> Choose a vehicle and its features.

- ☐ Decide if your vehicle is for people, objects, or both.
- ☐ Think about how your vehicle will move and the features it needs.
- ☐ Complete the information for your vehicle.

Vehicle: _____
Features on the control panel:
_____

Length: _____ cm
Weight: _____ kg
Fuel: _____
Top speed: _____ km per hour
Number of seats: _____
Number of lights: _____
Number of engines: _____

54 fifty-four

Step 3

Create

blueprint = plan

> Make a blueprint.

- [ ] Draw your vehicle from the front, the back, and the side.
- [ ] Add the information.
- [ ] Think of a name for your vehicle.
- [ ] Think about what your vehicle will do.

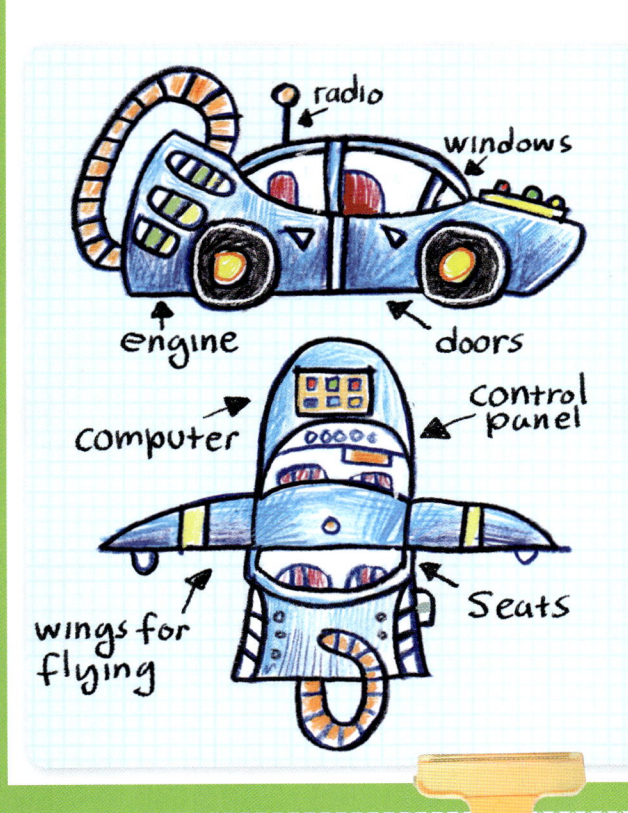

(blueprint drawing labeled: radio, windows, engine, doors, computer, control panel, seats, wings for flying)

Show your family your blueprint. Build your vehicle.

Step 4

Show and tell

> Present your vehicle.

- [ ] Share your vehicle drawing.
- [ ] Discuss details of your vehicle.
- [ ] Ask for improvements or suggestions for your vehicle.
- [ ] Find friends who chose the same vehicle type as you.

> The Amaxa is a new vehicle. It will fly and move on land. It will have a control panel.

> It will use water for fuel. It will get the water from the air.

Now I can ...

- ... describe space and the future.
- ... talk about the future using *will*.
- ... ask and answer about the future.
- ... write a brochure.

fifty-five 55

4 Dragons

How can I invent a story about a fantasy animal?

1 What do you know about dragons? Are they real?

2 Listen and complete. Not all words are used.

bad
Chinese
colorful
good
helpful
kind
lazy

NEW YEAR DRAGONS

_____ dragons **flew** through the streets for the _____ New Year celebration. People with sticks made the dragons move in the air. In Chinese culture, dragons bring _____ luck. They are **brave** and **strong**. And they are _____ and _____ to people.

3 Work with a partner. Think of two stories with dragons.

1 _____
2 _____

4 Act out the dragon routine with three friends.

CODE CRACKER

Step forwards ↑
Step backwards ↓
Step to the left ←
Step to the right →

Lift arms ↑
Lower arms ↓
Move arms to the left ←
Move arms to the right →

	Dancer 1	Dancer 2	Dancer 3	Dancer 4
Step 1	↑↑	↑↑	↑↑	↑↑
Step 2	→→	↑↑	↑↑	↑↑
Step 3	→↓	→→	↑↑	↑↑
Step 4	↑↑	→↓	→→	↑↑
Step 5	←←	↑↑	→↓	→→
Step 6	←↓	←←	→↓	→↓

Dragons around the world
VOCABULARY

I will learn words to describe dragons.

1 Listen and complete. Sing the song.

east   north   west

SONG TIME

Dragons in many lands

*Long, long ago there were dragons in many lands.
Some dragons were good. Other dragons were bad.*

The dragon from the **east** was **strong** and **brave**.
He **flew** in the sky and he made it rain.
Chorus

The dragon from the **west** was dangerous and bad.
He **burned** all the **villages** in the land.
Chorus

The dragon from the **north slept** in a cave.
He was **dangerous** and lazy and he wasn't very brave.
Chorus

Yellow dragon
Actions: swim, fly, walk, make rain
Qualities: brave, strong, good
Origin: _____

Green dragon
Actions: fly, swim, sleep
Qualities: lazy, dangerous, bad
Origin: _____

Red dragon
Actions: fly, walk, make fire, burn villages
Qualities: dangerous, strong, bad
Origin: _____

2 Read and complete.

1 The _____ dragon could swim. He wasn't brave.
2 The _____ dragon was dangerous. He couldn't swim.
3 The _____ dragon could walk. He wasn't dangerous.
4 The _____ dragon was strong. He couldn't swim.
5 The _____ dragon could swim. He wasn't lazy.
6 The _____ dragon was dangerous. He couldn't walk.

3 Create your own dragon.

Name: _____

Color: _____

Actions: _____

Qualities: _____

4 Play *Snap!*

"My dragon can make fire."

"Snap!"

5 Make your own picture dictionary. Draw and write the words in two groups: *Actions* and *Qualities*.

flew

swam

6 Listen and number. Then say.

My dragon

1. It flies with the clouds in the blue, blue sky.
2. It sleeps on the floor on a blanket of flowers.
3. It cleans clocks and glass plates in dark places.

a b c

7 Choose. Say it again as quickly as you can.

fifty-nine 59

Language lab
GRAMMAR: ACTIVITIES IN THE PAST

I will learn to talk about activities in the past.

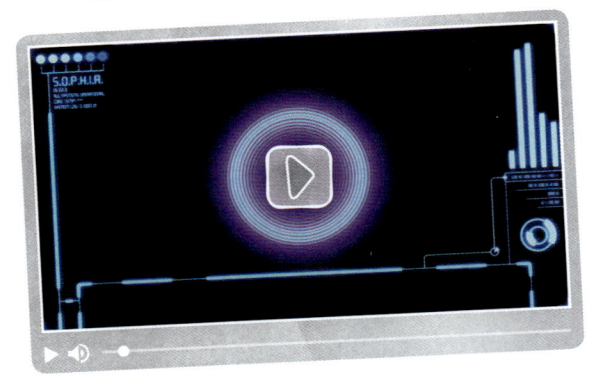

1 Watch the video.

> The dragon **was flying**.
> It **wasn't burning** a village.
> The dragons **were sleeping**.
> They **weren't eating**.
> **Was** the dragon **swimming**? Yes, it **was**.
> **Were** the dragons **eating**? No, they **weren't**.

2 Read and color the arrows.

Sunday

In the morning, …

… the blue dragon was swimming in the river.

… the green dragon was flying over the forest.

In the afternoon, …

… the green dragon was burning a village.

… the blue dragon was flying over the mountain.

In the evening, …

… both dragons were sleeping.

The blue dragon was sleeping in the sea.

The green dragon was sleeping on the beach.

afternoon | afternoon
morning | morning
evening | evening

Emilia looks for dragons. She follows clues from an old map.

3 Write sentences about the dragons. Ask and answer with partner.

What were the dragons doing at night?
1. The blue dragon _____ .
2. The green dragon _____ .
3. The dragons _____ .

4 Imagine you went with Emilia and complete.

morning   afternoon   evening   night

Time: _____   Place: _____   What were you doing? _____

5 Play the *Find a time* game.

CODE CRACKER

1. Ask a classmate, "What time do you have?"
2. If you have the same time, sit down. If you have a different time, ask another classmate.
3. How many classmates are left?

Make your own rule and play.

6 Draw the map and write labels. Ask and answer with friends.

Where were you?
At the beach.
What were you doing?
I was swimming.

In the morning

Diego was swimming at the beach.

Ana and Edu were eating breakfast.

Story lab
READING

I will read a story about good and bad dragons.

1 Look at the pictures. Is it a true story?

2 Read and listen.

A TALE OF TWO DRAGONS

1 Once upon a time, there was an island in the sea. One day, people were working in the fields. The sun was shining and there was one cloud in the sky. The cloud was a strange shape and it was moving towards the island. Soon, the cloud was very big. Then a small boy looked up.

"It's a fire dragon! Run to the beach!"

2 The fire dragon flew over the island. Soon, the trees in the forest were burning. Then the fire dragon flew towards the beach. A young girl shouted, "Go away!" She stamped her feet on the ground.

The fire dragon flew nearer. The people in the village were screaming, but the girl stamped her feet again. Then a friend joined her. Soon, all the children in the village were shouting and stamping their feet.

Values Be the best you can.

3 Use the words to describe the characters.

bad   brave   dangerous   good   lazy   scared   strong

The girl was brave because she shouted at the dragon.

3 At the bottom of the sea, a water dragon was sleeping. The noise from the beach woke it up.

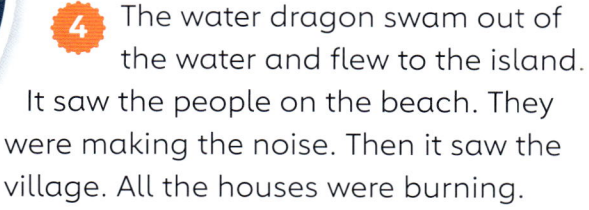

4 The water dragon swam out of the water and flew to the island. It saw the people on the beach. They were making the noise. Then it saw the village. All the houses were burning.

5 The water dragon made rain from the clouds to put out the fires. Then it flew after the fire dragon. At the top of the mountain, the water dragon pushed the fire dragon into a cave and made a door with a big rock.

6 The people of the village still remember the fire dragon. They can see its smoke at the top of the mountain. And when the fire dragon is angry, burning rocks come out of the top of the mountain.

4 What was the story about? Read and check ✓.

1. It is a story about technology in the future. ☐
2. It is a story about real events. ☐
3. It is a story with fantasy events. ☐

> Fantasy stories are adventures with magical animals and people in a strange world.

5 Read the sentences and write *real* or *fantasy*.

1. Rain clouds put out fires. _____
2. There are water dragons at the bottom of the sea. _____
3. Fire burns trees. _____
4. There are dragons inside mountains. _____
5. Some mountains have smoke coming out the top. _____
6. Dragons can change the weather. _____

6 Act out the story in groups.

Experiment lab
SCIENCE: FLYING MACHINES

I will learn how to make a paper airplane.

1 Look, read, and write **bi-plane** or **jet plane**.

Watch a video about bi-planes.

The first airplane with an engine flew at the start of the 20th century. Now, there are lots of different types of airplanes.

1. This airplane has a propeller. _____
2. This airplane has lots of windows. _____
3. This airplane has two wings on each side. _____
4. This airplane has two engines. _____
5. This airplane has wheels under the wings. _____
6. This airplane has two wheels. _____

propeller / engine — **bi-plane**

engines — **jet plane**

2 Read, listen, and complete.

push lift weight pull

How does an airplane stay in the air?

1 _____ 2 _____ 3 _____ 4 _____

The engine pushes the airplane forward.

The air moves over the wings and lifts the airplane up.

The air pulls the airplane backwards. This is called air resistance.

The weight of the airplane pulls it towards the ground.

When an airplane is flying, the push is equal to the pull and the lift is equal to the weight.

3 Look and read. Discuss with a partner.

Airplanes have a special shape to make a small amount of air resistance. We call it a *streamlined* shape. Which airplane is streamlined?

sixty-four

4 Read and answer.

MATH ZONE

Imagine a jet plane is flying at 12 kilometers above ground. It uses about 4 liters of fuel every second.

1. How much fuel does it use in an hour?
   _____

Now imagine it is flying at 9 kilometers above ground. It uses about 4.5 liters of fuel every second.

2. How much fuel does it use in an hour?
   _____

5 Answer the questions. Discuss with a partner.

An airplane uses more fuel when it is nearer the ground.

Does the weight of the airplane change?

Does the air resistance change?

EXPERIMENT TIME

What model of airplane flies best?

Basic airplane = B

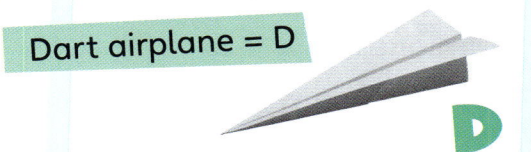

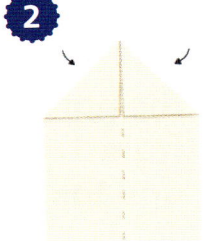

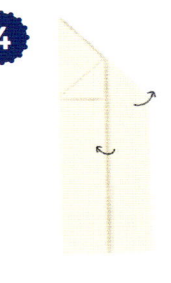

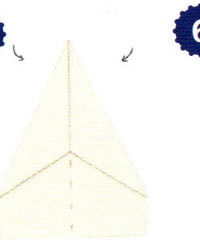

Dart airplane = D

To make a Basic airplane, follow the instructions labeled **B**. To make a Dart airplane, follow the instructions labeled **D**.

1. Fold a piece of paper in half and open it again. B D
2. Fold the top corners to the center line. B D
3. Fold the paper in half. B
4. Fold the edges up. B D
5. Fold the corner edges to the center line. D
6. Fold the wings back. D

1. Throw your airplanes three times.
2. Record the results.

	Basic airplane	Dart airplane
Distance	1 _____ 2 _____ 3 _____	1 _____ 2 _____ 3 _____
Time in air	1 _____ 2 _____ 3 _____	1 _____ 2 _____ 3 _____

sixty-five 65

Events in the past
COMMUNICATION

I will ask and answer about events in the past.

STOLEN
There was a fire at a party. Someone stole a dragon statue.

What **were** you **doing** when the fire **started**?
I **was swimming** in the pool when the fire **started**.
I **wasn't eating** when the fire **started**.

1 Read and number.

When the fire started, …
1 … some people were sitting down.
2 … a man was swimming in the pool.
3 … some children were flying paper airplanes.
4 … a woman was eating a sandwich.
5 … a woman was burning leaves.
6 … a man was painting a wall.

2 Imagine you were at the party. Choose an activity from 1. Interview your friends and take notes.

When the fire started, what were you doing?

Witness 1 Name:

Witness 2 Name:

Witness 3 Name:

Witness 4 Name:

What were you doing when the fire started?
I was swimming.
I wasn't swimming. I was flying an airplane.
So was I! We were flying airplanes.
I was eating a sandwich.

Writing lab
A WITNESS STATEMENT

I will learn to write a witness statement.

1 Read and complete.

> brave   matches   morning   statue   swimming   talking

The local police interviewed all the witnesses from the party.

WITNESS STATEMENT

Crime: Stolen dragon statue   **Date of crime:** April 17th   **Witness Name:** Edu Lopes

STATEMENT

☐ I arrived at the house at 9 in the _____ . ☐ I was _____ to my friend when the fire started. ☐ I saw some _____ near the _____ . ☐ I'm not very _____ . I ran away from the fire. ☐ When the police arrived, I was _____ in the pool.

Signature: *Edu Lopes*

2 Read and number the sentences in 1.

1. Did you see anything strange?
2. When did you arrive at the party?
3. What were you doing when the police arrived?
4. What were you doing when the fire started?
5. What did you do when you saw the fire?

3 Look at your notes from page 66 Activity 2. Then write a witness statement.

4 Who stole the dragon? Discuss in groups then listen and check ✓.

- The man swimming. ☐
- The man painting. ☐
- The woman eating a sandwich. ☐
- The woman burning leaves. ☐

> A witness statement is like a journal. Remember to write facts and write a lot of detail.

sixty-seven

PROJECT AND REVIEW

Invent and tell a story about a fantasy animal

Step 1
Research

> Find out about fantasy animals in stories from your country.

- ☐ Research fantasy animals.
- ☐ Choose one of the animals.
- ☐ Make a list of its qualities and actions.
- ☐ Find a picture.

Cipactli

Qualities: hungry, dangerous, bad
Actions: swim, fly
Origin: Mexico

Step 2
Plan

> Invent your fantasy animal and make a story outline.

- ☐ Invent details about your fantasy animal and take notes—its name, where it lived, and what it was like.
- ☐ Then write a story outline using the example words below.
- ☐ Then fold the piece of paper in six strips.

_____

met _____

at / in _____.

It was _____.

It was _____.

Then they _____.

68 sixty-eight

Step 3

Create

> ✈ Invent a story with your friends.

- ☐ Work in groups. Use your outline.
- ☐ Write the name of your fantasy animal at the top of your paper.
- ☐ Fold the paper over the writing. Pass the paper to your left.
- ☐ Write who your fantasy animal met.
- ☐ Continue to fold and pass the paper after you answer each question.
- ☐ Open the paper. Use the notes and draw an illustration for the story.

Cipactli

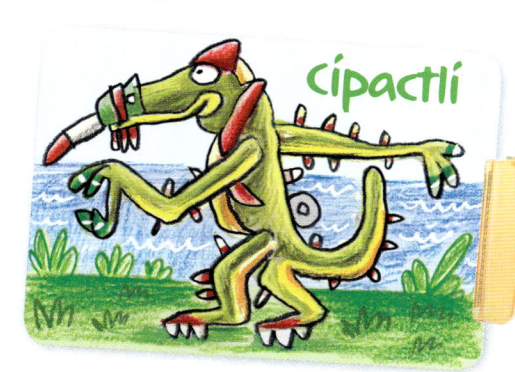

What was your fantasy animal doing when it met a friend?
What was the friend doing?
What did they do next?

Show your family the illustration and tell them the story.

Step 4

Show and tell

> ✈ Tell your story to your friends.

- ☐ Use the story outline and your drawing.
- ☐ Add details and tell your story.

> The Cipactli was very strong. It lived in the north by a river. One day, the Cipactli met the Chupacabras. It was eating supper when it saw the Chupacabras.

Now I can ...

- ... use words to describe dragons.
- ... talk about activities in the past.
- ... ask and answer about events in the past.
- ... write a witness statement.

sixty-nine 69

2 Checkpoint
UNITS 3 AND 4

G	G yesterday	visited	A was using	A will sleep
last year	W+	A	A two days ago	A
didn't fly	won't use	flew	A +E	A tomorrow
G next week	wasn't using	in the afternoon	A	G wasn't playing
A	G played	in the morning	G	
	will use	A slept	next year	A won't play
	G will fly	didn't sleep		will play
G N+				

seventy

1 🎧 034 **Listen and write Z in the squares.**

Zoe

2 **Read and check ✓ the true sentences.**

G = George
A = Antonio

Antonio   George

1 George played in the space station yesterday.
2 He wasn't playing with the control panel.
3 He won't fly north next week.
4 Antonio slept in the village two days ago.
5 He wasn't using the radio.
6 He won't play with the screen tomorrow.

3 **Complete the squares on the board. Then write a sentence.**

🟨 = actions
🟦 = objects and places
⬜ = times

Zoe _____
_____ _____ .

4 **Write about yourself.**

I _____ _____ _____ .
I _____ _____ _____ .
I _____ _____ _____ .
I _____ _____ _____ .

5 💬 **Imagine you are at the space station. Ask and answer with a partner.**

Did you visit the village last year?
No, I didn't.

Were you playing with a screen in the morning?
No, I wasn't.

Will you fly north tomorrow?
Yes, I will!

Where will you sleep next week?
I will sleep in the space station!

Test your progress with English Benchmark Young Learners

seventy-one 71

Guna Yala
CULTURE

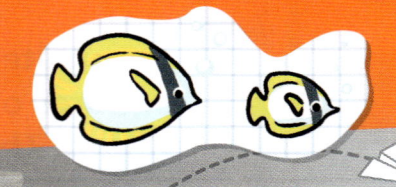

1 Read. How many islands in Guna Yala don't have houses?

Panama

Panama is the most southern country in Central America. In Panama, people speak Spanish.

Visit the Guna Yala archipelago

The Guna Yala archipelago has more than 300 islands. It is in the Caribbean sea, 90 kilometers north of the coast of Panama. The Guna people live on 40 of the islands and speak their own language.

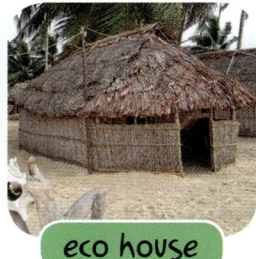

Guna Yala   coral reef   eco house

2 Read, listen, and match.

Fun Fact!
There are over 1500 islands off the coast of Panama.

In every Guna village there is a community hall where people meet and listen to traditional stories and songs. Guna people care for their environment and there are special rules for visitors.

Visitors will stay …   … plastic bags on the island of Digir.
They won't stay …   … in big hotels.
Visitors won't use …   … in beach huts.
Visitors won't see …   … computers.
Visitors will see …   … beautiful beaches and coral reefs.

3 Read and complete.

bigger   dangerous
flew   flying
moon   shouted
was   wasn't   were

THE GRANDCHILDREN OF THE _____

One night, a dragon _____ over Guna Yala. Most people _____ sleeping, but one boy _____ collecting branches. The sun was _____ for his skin. When the boy saw the dragon, it was _____ towards the moon! Soon it was eating the moon. The moon was getting smaller and it _____ shining. The boy _____ and shot arrows at the dragon. The dragon stopped, and the moon got _____ again. In modern times, when there is a lunar eclipse, there is a special ceremony for the Guna people with white skin and hair.

4 Read and complete the meanings of the symbols.

The Guna people make "molas" for their clothes. Many molas have pictures from nature like fish or birds. Guna people fill the empty spaces in the molas with symbols. The triangles are huts. The bars are rays of sunlight. The zig-zags are dangerous teeth. The maze is a trap for dangerous animals.

▲ triangle = _____
≡ bar = _____
∧∧∧ zig-zags = _____
⊐ maze = _____

My Culture

5 What do the symbols mean? What symbols do you have in your culture? Discuss with a partner.

6 Make a paper mola.

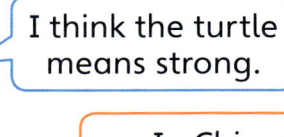

I think the turtle means strong.

In Chinese culture, a panda means friendship.

seventy-three 73

5 Endangered animals

How can I organize a campaign to save an animal?

Endangered animals = there aren't many of these animals living on Earth.

1 Why is wildlife endangered? Discuss with a partner.

We cut down trees to make paper.

2 🎧 036 Listen, count, complete, and circle the habitat.

Ottery Wildlife Center — Observation notes

Animal: Otters
Habitat: They live in and around the water.
  forest   river   field
Threat: Water pollution in the rivers and seas.
Time: _____

Animal: Butterflies
Habitat: They live on flowers.
  forest   river   field
Threat: Chemicals on plants.
Time: _____

Animal: Owls
Habitat: They live in trees.
  forest   river   field
Threat: Loss of habitat.
Time: _____

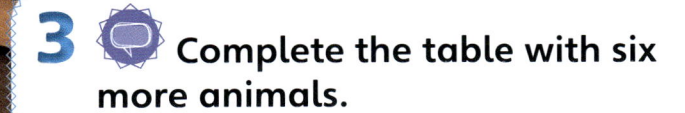

3 💬 Complete the table with six more animals.

animal	habitat	threat
otters	river	pollution
bats	forest	chemicals

4 💬 Why are the animals endangered? Discuss with a partner.

Loss of habitat endangers bats.

Wonderful wildlife
VOCABULARY

I will learn animal and habitat words.

1 Listen and match. Sing the song.

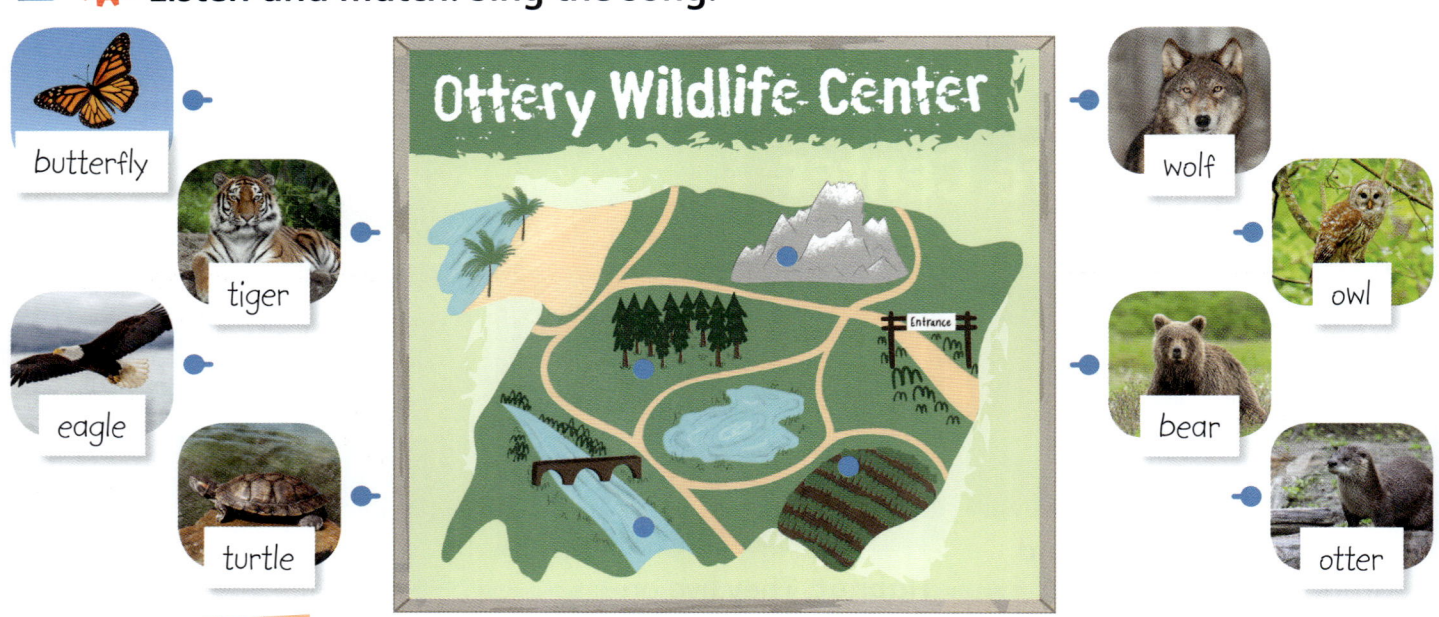

butterfly · tiger · eagle · turtle

Ottery Wildlife Center

wolf · owl · bear · otter

SONG TIME

🦋 Habitats

Habitat! Habitat! What is that?
There are **butterflies** in the field.
There are **tigers** in the forest.
There are **eagles** in the mountains.
There are **turtles** in the river.
They are habitats!
The animals' habitats! Habitats.

There are **wolves** in the **field**.
There are owls in the forest.
There are bears in the **mountains**.
There are **otters** in the river.
They are habitats!
The animals' habitats! Habitats.

2 Draw your route on the map in **1**. Then ask and answer with a partner.

You are going to visit the Ottery Wildlife Center on the weekend. You will see four different animals at four different places.

Where will you go first?

To the mountains.

You'll see eagles and bears there.

3 Look at your friends' routes. Whose route is the most similar to yours? Complete the table.

| Key | Field = F | Forest = F |
| | Mountain = M | River = R |

Me	Friend:	Friend:	Friend:
__	__	__	__
__	__	__	__
__	__	__	__
__	__	__	__
__	__	__	__

CODE CRACKER

I'll go to the river, the mountains, and then to the fields.

I won't.

Your route is the most similar to mine.

I'll go to the fields, too.

4 Make your own picture dictionary. Label the animals and their habitats.

forest
owl
tiger

5 🅿🅷 038 ▶ **Listen and complete. Then say.**

brown   cranky   dreamy   friendly
gray   green   prissy   triangular

A _____ grouse, a _____ crab, a _____ frog, a _____ dragon, a _____ princess, a _____ bridge, a _____ tree, and _____ grass growing all around.

I'm going to read you a story.

What's it about?

6 🅿🅷 ▶ **Say it again as quickly as you can.**

Well, it's about …

Language lab
GRAMMAR: *IF* ... SENTENCES

I will learn to use sentences with if.

1 Watch the video.

> If they **destroy** the forest, there **won't be** any wildlife.
> If they **don't clean up** the river, the fish **will die**.
> If they **build** a lot more houses, it **will be** very noisy.
> If they **don't care** for the wildlife, it **won't be** a beautiful place.

2 What will change? Read and discuss with a partner.

"There will be a lot more new houses."

"But there won't be many trees."

Wolf Forest

Wolf Forest Project 2033

We will build a hundred and fifty new houses. There will be a train station with a parking lot. There will be a new school and a shopping mall. There will be a new sports center and swimming pool.

3 Look at 2. Who are the changes good for and not good for? Discuss with a partner.

"There will be a lot more houses. That's good for people."

"But there won't be a forest. That isn't good for the wildlife."

4 Make sentences with a partner.

If they cut down the forest,
If they build a sports center,
If they move the river,
If there is a shopping center,
If there is a train station,

there will be a lot of traffic.
they will need a parking lot.
there won't be a river.
there won't be any fields or flowers.
they will destroy the wildlife habitat.

If they cut down the forest, they will destroy the wildlife habitat.

5 Choose two ideas and complete. Then discuss with friends.

- An enormous campsite on the beach. ☐
- The new train line will go **through the forest.** ☐
- A sports center and swimming pool for **Wolf Forest Project.** ☐
- The new shopping mall will bring a lot more stores. ☐

What are you worried about?
I'm worried about the new sports center.
Why?
If they build the new sports center, there won't be a forest.

If they build a _____ , _____ .
If they build a _____ , _____ .

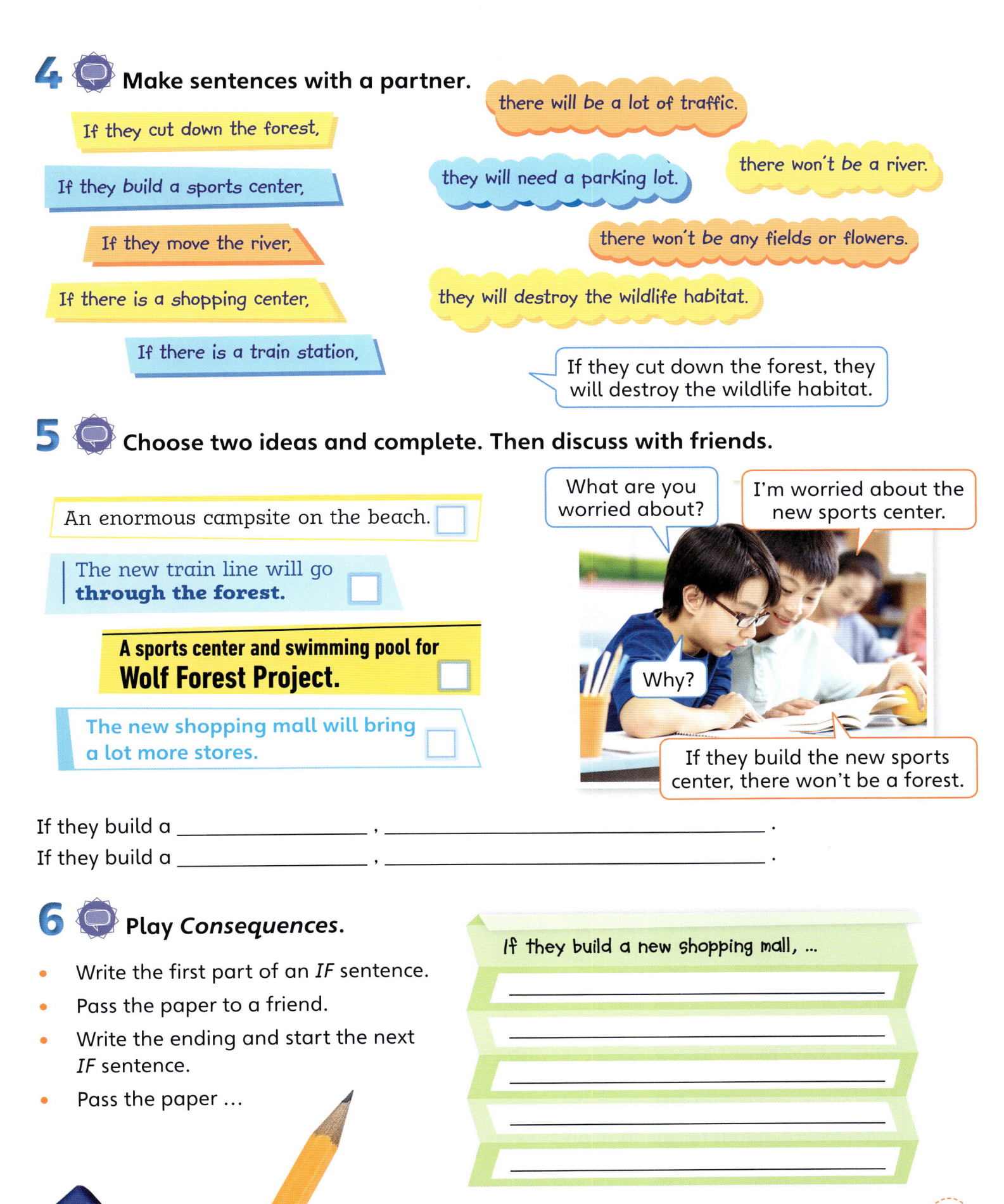

6 Play *Consequences*.

- Write the first part of an *IF* sentence.
- Pass the paper to a friend.
- Write the ending and start the next *IF* sentence.
- Pass the paper …

If they build a new shopping mall, …
_____
_____
_____
_____
_____

Story lab
READING

I will read a story about caring for animals.

1 Look at the pictures. What happens?

2 🎧 Read and listen.

Aset and Kara 🐾

1 Aset was walking in the forest when he heard a sound coming from a bush. He looked under the bush and found a little gray puppy. Aset decided to keep the puppy. "I will call you Kara," he whispered to the puppy. He took Kara back to the farm and found a warm place in the barn for a bed. Soon, Kara was asleep.

2 Every day, Aset cleaned the barn and fed Kara. After, they played with an old teddy bear and a rope. Aset ran round the barn pulling the teddy bear on the rope. Kara chased the toy. It was Kara's favorite game! Kara and Aset were soon best friends, but nobody knew Aset's secret.

One day, Mom opened the barn door and saw Kara. "A wolf! There's a wolf in the barn!" she screamed. Aset tried to explain, "She isn't a wolf. She's Kara, my puppy." But Dad knew that Kara was a wolf and he was very worried. "I saw a wolf walking around the fields," he said. "It was probably Kara's mother. If we keep Kara on the farm, her mother won't go back to the forest."

Values Care for wild animals.

3 Why can't Aset keep Kara as a pet? Check ✓ three reasons.

1. His parents don't like wolves. ☐
2. Wolves are wild animals. ☐
3. It will be dangerous for the farm animals. ☐
4. Kara needs to be with her mother. ☐
5. Kara doesn't like Aset. ☐

3 The next day, Aset and his father took Kara back to the forest. He knew he couldn't keep the wolf cub. It was dangerous for the farm animals, but he was sad. Aset left Kara by the bush where he found her. Then they waited quietly.

"Awooo!" Kara called.

"She's calling for her mother," explained Dad. "If you are quiet, you will see her." Suddenly, a big, beautiful wolf appeared. She ran to Kara and licked her. Then they disappeared into the forest.

4 That night, Aset went to the barn with his mom. They were filling a basket with apples when Aset heard a soft sound. It was a little gray puppy wagging its tail. "Thank you, Mom!" He said. "I will call her …"

4 Why does Aset think Kara is a puppy? Discuss with a partner.

> I think Aset doesn't know what a wolf cub looks like.

5 Read and write the character's name next to each thought.

1. If I take Kara home, I will have my own pet. _____
2. If I keep Kara in the barn, my parents won't know. _____
3. If I look in the barn, I will see Aset's hard work. _____
4. If I put Kara near the same bush, her mother will come and find her. _____
5. If the mother finds Kara, she won't stay near the farm. _____
6. If we get Aset a puppy, he will be very happy. _____ _____

6 Act out the story in groups.

Experiment lab
ART AND DESIGN: LIGHT BOXES

I will learn how to make an animal light box.

1 Read and complete. playing   X-rays   movies

We use light boxes for many different things. Doctors and vets use them to see _____ of bones. Animators use them to make pictures for _____ . Children use them for _____ and learning. We can also use light boxes to make beautiful artworks.

▶ Watch a video about 2D and 3D shapes.

2 Read, listen, and complete.

Light box art

Light box artworks are very interesting because they are three dimensional (or 3D). Solid objects are 3D. They have **height**, **width**, and **depth**. They have different faces. Paintings and drawings are two dimensional (or 2D). They have height and width, but they don't have depth and they only have one face.

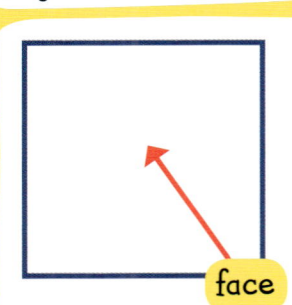

This is a _____ dimensional artwork. It has _____ face(s).

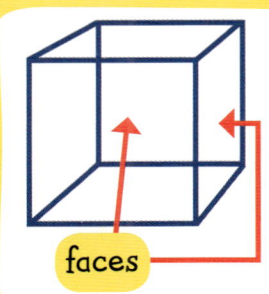

This is a _____ dimensional artwork. It has _____ face(s).

3 Write the number of faces.

MATH ZONE

1. 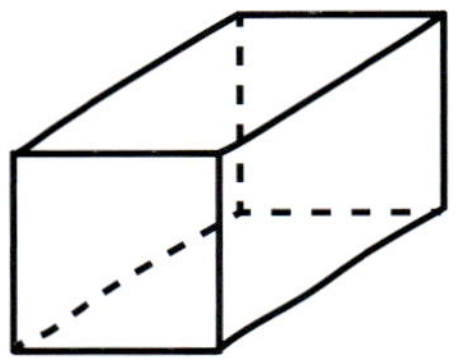
2. 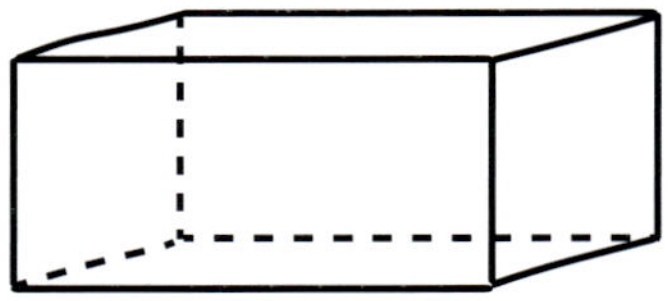
3. 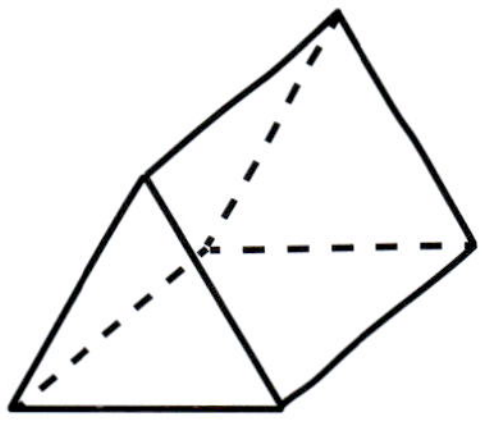
4.

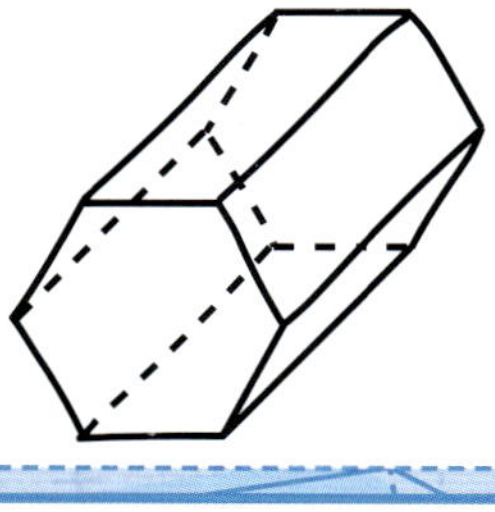

82 eighty-two

4 Sometimes the images inside light boxes are positive and negative shapes. Complete the pattern of this light box design.

5 Write a code for your pattern.

Make a letter key for the colors and a number key for the animal footprints.

Write the code starting with the letter for the color, then the number for the footprint and then *p* for positive and *n* for negative.

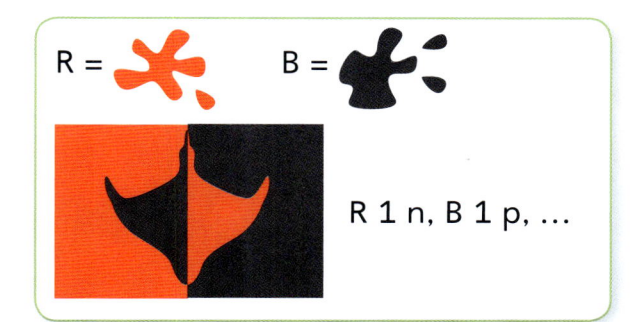

R =
B =

R 1 n, B 1 p, …

EXPERIMENT TIME

Can you make an animal light box?

Materials

- 4 pieces of white cardboard – 30 cm × 20 cm
- 4 strips of foam board – 2 × 30 cm × 5 cm and 2 × 20 cm × 5 cm
- 12 strips of thick cardboard 6 × 20 cm and 6 × 30 cm
- 1 strip of LED lights – 1 m
- ruler, pencil, scissors, glue

1. Glue the four strips of foam board to form a box.
2. Draw and cut out the background and animals for the light box using 3 of the pieces of cardboard.
3. Layer and glue the three cut out drawings with the strips of cardboard in between each.
4. Put your 3D picture inside the box. Glue the LED strip inside the box behind the pictures. Cut a hole in the last piece of white cardboard. Glue the cardboard to the back of the box.
5. Pull the cable of the LED outside the light box through the hole. Switch on the lights!

eighty-three

More or fewer?
COMMUNICATION

*I will describe quantities using **more** and **fewer**.*

1 🎧 041 💬 **Listen and say *true* or *false*.**

There are **fewer** bears **than** wolves.
There are **more** owls **than** otters.

Animals in forest

Season: Spring **Ranger:** Julia Holden

- otters 15
- eagles 24
- owls 17
- wolves 32
- bears 6

2 💬 **Look at 1 and make your own bar chart with three animals. Then ask and answer with a partner.**

Visitor:
- How many wolves are there?
- Are there more wolves than eagles?
- Are there fewer eagles than otters?

Ranger:
- There are thirty-two.
- Yes, there are.
- No, there aren't. There are more.

3 Look at your bar chart. Complete the sentences.

1. There are fewer _____ than _____ .
3. There are more _____ than _____ .
2. There are fewer _____ than _____ .
4. There are more _____ than _____ .

Writing lab
A LETTER

I will learn to write a letter.

1 What does Jack want? Read and check ✓. Then number the features.

a new airport ☐   a solution ☐
more rabbits ☐   a new forest ☐

① = the date
② = the person writing the letter
③ = the person receiving the letter
④ = the address
⑤ = the problem
⑥ = the solution

> When you write a formal letter, be polite. Remember to add the correct start and end.

☐ 73 Highlands Road
Oxbo, Wisconsin 54552
☐ April 11th
☐ Dear Ms. Tamer,
☐ Some people want to destroy the forest and build an airport. This forest is a habitat for many wolves. If they destroy the forest, the wolves will leave the forest. If the wolves leave the forest, there will be more rabbits. This won't be good for our forest.
☐ Please build the airport in a different place. Please don't destroy the forest.
Kind regards,
☐ Jack Robers

2 Read and answer.

1. What will happen if they destroy the forest? _____
2. What will happen if the wolves leave the forest? _____
3. What will happen if there are more rabbits in the forest? _____

3 Complete the code. Then use the words to write a letter.

CODE CRACKER

If they 🟠 🟣, they will destroy the 🔵.
If they destroy the 🔵, the 🟢, will have no habitat.
If the 🟢 have no habitat, they will leave.
If the 🟢 leave, there will be 🔴 🟡.
This is bad for our 🔵.

○ = build / plant
○ = maize / houses
○ = fields / pond
○ = otters / butterflies
○ = more / fewer
○ = fish / flowers

PROJECT AND REVIEW

Organize a campaign to save an animal

Step 1

Research

> Find out about endangered animals.

- [ ] Where do these animals live?
- [ ] Find out which habitat they live in.
- [ ] Find out why the animals are endangered.

animals	places	habitats	threats
panda	China	forest	loss of habitat
orangutan	Indonesia	rainforest	loss of habitat

Step 2

Plan

> Think about different actions for a campaign.

- [ ] Choose one of the animals.
- [ ] In groups, choose one action each.
- [ ] List the tasks for your actions.
- [ ] Make a list of materials.

Campaign actions
A poster with pictures and information
A letter to a newspaper
A quiz competition

A quiz competition.
Collect information.
Write ten questions.
Find pictures to illustrate quiz.

The Orangutan Quiz
1 Where do orangutans come from?
   a Iceland   b Indonesia   c Ireland
2 What kind of animals are they?
   a Fish   b Birds   c Mammals

Step 3

Create

> Prepare the campaign.

- [ ] Prepare your campaign action.
- [ ] Write, draw, or make your action.
- [ ] In your group, look at your actions together.
- [ ] Decide how to present your campaign.

Tell your family about your campaign and ask them to do the quiz.

Step 4

Show and tell

> Present the campaign.

- [ ] Present your campaign.
- [ ] Talk to your classmates for 5 minutes about your campaign.
- [ ] Display your campaigns.
- [ ] Use counters to vote for the best.
- [ ] Give 5 counters to the first, 3 to the second, and 2 to the third.
- [ ] The campaign with the most counters is the winner.

The winner of the endangered animals campaign is Save the Orangutans!

Now I can …

- … use animal and habitat words.
- … use sentences with *if*.
- … describe quantities with *more* and *fewer*.
- … write a letter.

eighty-seven 87

6 Join in!

How can I have a club fair?

Children's Day

1 What are the children doing? How do they know each other?

2 Listen and complete.

April 23rd   April 30th   June 1st

Many countries all over the world have a special day for children. In China, Children's Day is on _____ . In Turkey, it's on _____ and in Mexico it's on _____ . The date is different, but the idea is the same. In all the countries, groups of children **take part in** a day of celebrations. Children perform in **choirs** and take part in **chess contests**.

3 **Classify the activities and add more.**

art exhibition   chess   dance   gymnastics
singing   soccer   table tennis   volleyball

Sports	Culture
_____	_____
_____	_____
_____	_____
_____	_____
_____	_____

4 Write two activities you like and find friends with the same activities.

CODE CRACKER

Do you like dance?

Yes, I do!

5 **Talk about your friends.**

Six of my friends like to dance. We can make a dance group.

eighty-nine 89

Join a club!
VOCABULARY

I will learn club activity words.

1 Listen and number. Sing the song.

SONG TIME

Join our club!

Come and join our clubs! You'll have lots of fun.
Oh, the **neighborhood** clubs are the number one!

There are ten in the **choir** and we **practice** a lot.
We **get better** and better. Together we're hot!

You'll **take part in contests** and you'll **cheer** the team.
When the **ice-skating** club wins, it's a real dream!

Drama club **meets** every week and we have a great time.
You'll **make new friends** who are funny and kind.

Come and join our clubs! You'll have lots of fun.
Oh, the neighborhood clubs are the number one!

2 Read and match.

Fred   Lily   Sam   Eva

Sam is in a lot of clubs and he has a lot of friends!

He is in the choir with Eva. She's a neighborhood friend.

He's in the drama club with Lily. She's a school friend.

And he's in a soccer club with his cousin, Fred.

3 💬 Have a class vote for the favorite club.

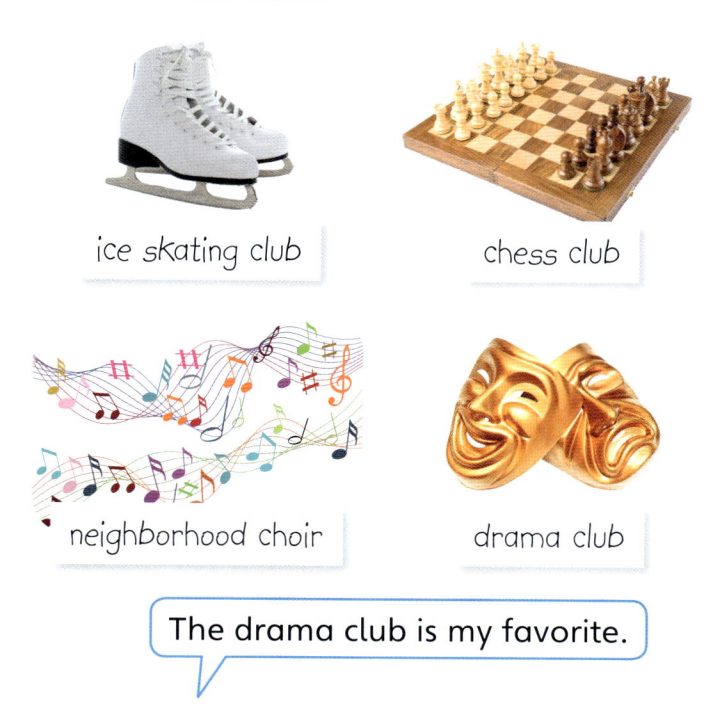

ice skating club

chess club

neighborhood choir

drama club

The drama club is my favorite.

4 💬 Choose a club and who you will go with. Then ask and answer with a partner.

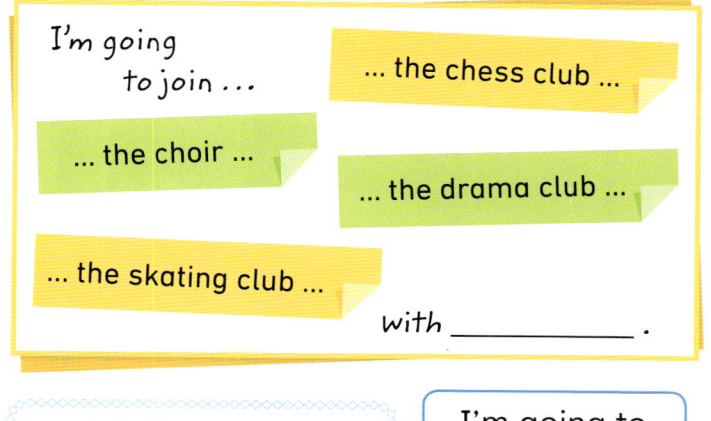

I'm going to join …
… the chess club …
… the choir …
… the drama club …
… the skating club …
with _____ .

a club friend   family
a neighborhood friend
a school friend

I'm going to join the drama club with Jack.

Who's Jack?

He's a school friend.

5 🌿 Make your own picture dictionary. Draw and write the words in two groups: *Actions* and *Activities*.

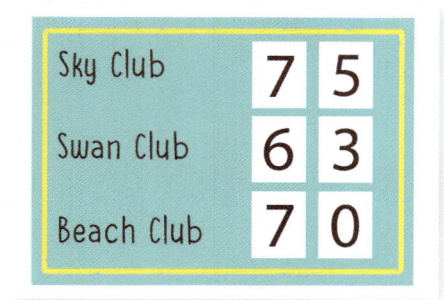

choir

cheer

6 Ph 🔧 ▶ Listen and circle. Then say.

Sky Club	7	5
Swan Club	6	3
Beach Club	7	0

1 Sweet / Swan school's ice-skating team has the smallest score.

2 Stand up in the snow and stop / start smiling.

3 Spaces with snow / snails are special in Spain.

7 Ph ▶ Choose. Say it as quickly as you can.

Language lab
GRAMMAR: *SHOULD, ALWAYS, OR NEVER*

I will learn to talk about rules using should.

1 Watch the video.

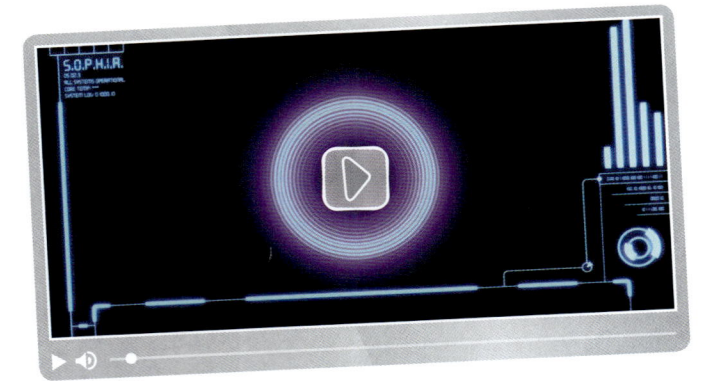

> You **should** tidy the space.
> You **shouldn't** push your friends.

> Alice **always** tidies the chairs.
> Alice **often** takes out the equipment.
> Jim **sometimes** tidies the chairs.
> Jim **never** takes out the equipment.

2 Read and check ✓ or cross ✗.

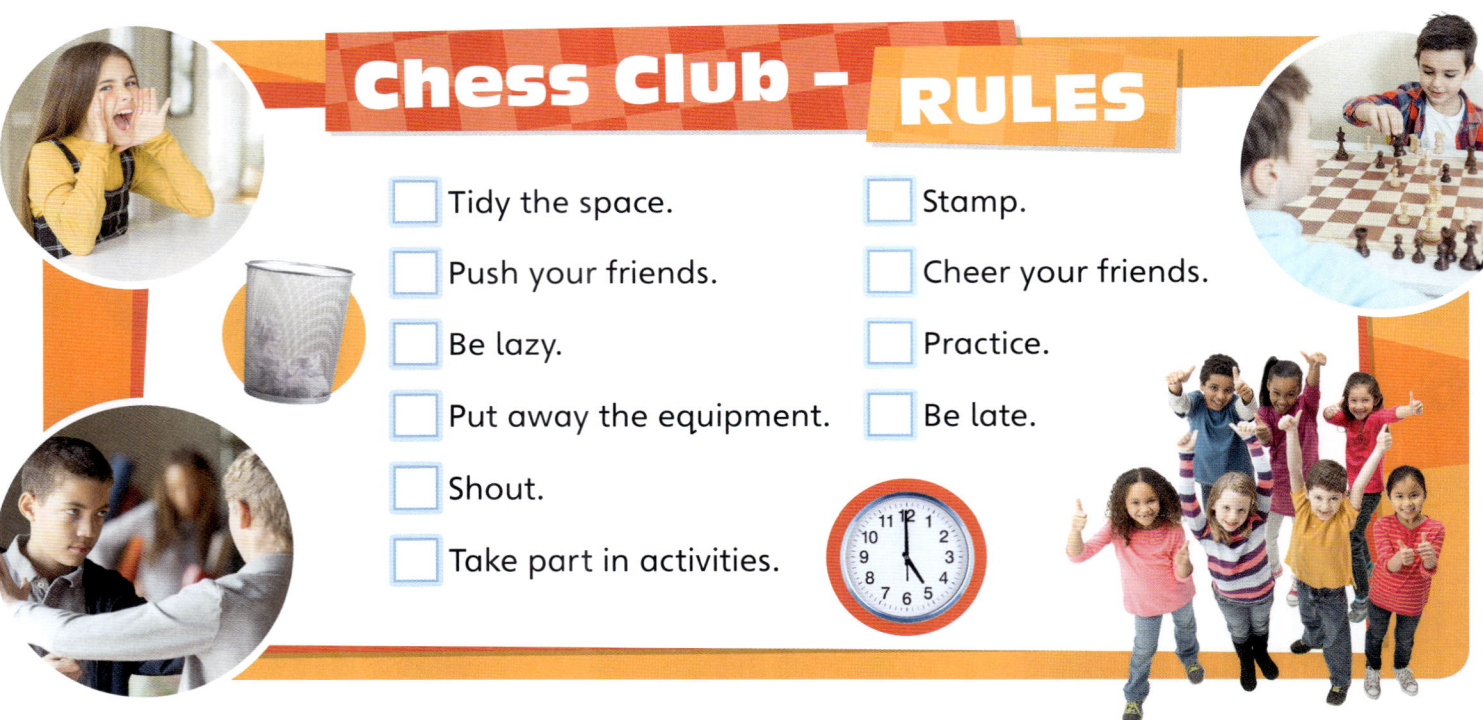

Chess Club – RULES

- ☐ Tidy the space.
- ☐ Push your friends.
- ☐ Be lazy.
- ☐ Put away the equipment.
- ☐ Shout.
- ☐ Take part in activities.
- ☐ Stamp.
- ☐ Cheer your friends.
- ☐ Practice.
- ☐ Be late.

3 Discuss the rules with a partner.

> You shouldn't be late.

> You should tidy the space.

4 Choose a place and make a poster with rules.

classroom   library   park   playground

5 Look, read, and complete.

Club Tasks – Week 3	When you do a task, put a check mark by your name.			
	Tidy chairs	Put away equipment	Empty trash	Take out equipment
Alice	✓✓✓✓✓		✓✓	✓✓✓✓
Jim	✓✓	✓✓✓✓✓	✓✓✓✓	

1 _____ always puts away the equipment.
2 _____ sometimes empties the trash.
3 _____ often empties the trash.
4 _____ never puts away the equipment.

We go to an art club.

6 Create your own key. Then complete the table for you and a partner. Tell a new partner your results.

Key
always = ♥
often =
sometimes =
never =

What club do you go to?
I go to a table tennis club.
How do you help?
I often put away the equipment.

CODE CRACKER

Tasks	My club: _____	My partner's club: _____
Tidy the space		
Take out equipment		
Empty the trash		
Put away equipment		
Close the windows		
Clean the floor		

7 Complete the sentences.

always   never

1 You should _____ arrive on time.
2 You should _____ be lazy.
3 You should _____ take part in activities.
4 You should _____ push your friends.

ninety-three 93

Story lab
READING

I will read a story about a vacation adventure.

1 Look at the pictures. What time of year is it?

New friends

2 Read and listen.

1 It was the winter vacation and the city was full of lights and people. Everyone was going out and having fun, but I couldn't join in. I was going to my grandma's village because Mom and Dad were working. "You'll have a great time, Maryam!" Mom said. But I didn't believe her.

All my friends are in the city!

TO: SCHOOL FRIENDS
SEE YOU ALL NEXT MONTH
:C :(

2 The first morning I was really bored. "Go and buy some bread for lunch," Grandma said. I was looking at my phone when I came out of the shop, and I bumped into a boy about my age.

Oh! Excuse me!

That's OK.

3 We started talking. His name was Oliver and he didn't live in the village. "I'm from a city to the north," he said. "I sometimes come here for my vacation."

I love it here!

But what do you do all day?

"I always go ice skating with my friends," Oliver said. "You should come, too." "I can't skate," I explained. "You'll learn!" Oliver answered.

Values Make new friends.

3 Work with a partner and answer the questions.

1. Who is telling the story?
3. How does she make new friends?
2. How does Maryam feel at the start of the story? Why?
4. How does she learn to skate?

4 After lunch, Grandma found a pair of old ice skates. "Your mom often went skating," she said. "You should wear this helmet, as well."

The next day, I joined Oliver and his friends, and we went to the frozen river. At first, I couldn't stand up, but Oliver helped me. I practiced, and I got better. "You have good balance," Oliver said. The next day, I joined Oliver and the other kids, and we skated to an old bridge. I loved it!

5 The rest of the month was great. I made new friends, and at the end of the month I took part in the village ice skating competition. I didn't win, but my new friends and Grandma all cheered! I never want to be in the city for my vacation again!

4 When does it happen? Read and complete.

1. Maryam learns how to skate.
2. Maryam goes to her Grandma's village.
3. Maryam takes part in an ice skating competition.
4. Maryam meets Oliver.

B = Beginning
M = Middle
E = End

5 Write a story summary.

Title: _____
Main characters: _____
Place: _____
At the beginning: _____
Then: _____
At the end: _____

6 Act out the story in groups.

Experiment lab
SCIENCE: SPORTS AND THE SENSES

I will learn how to balance using my senses.

1 What skills do you need for ice hockey? Read and underline.

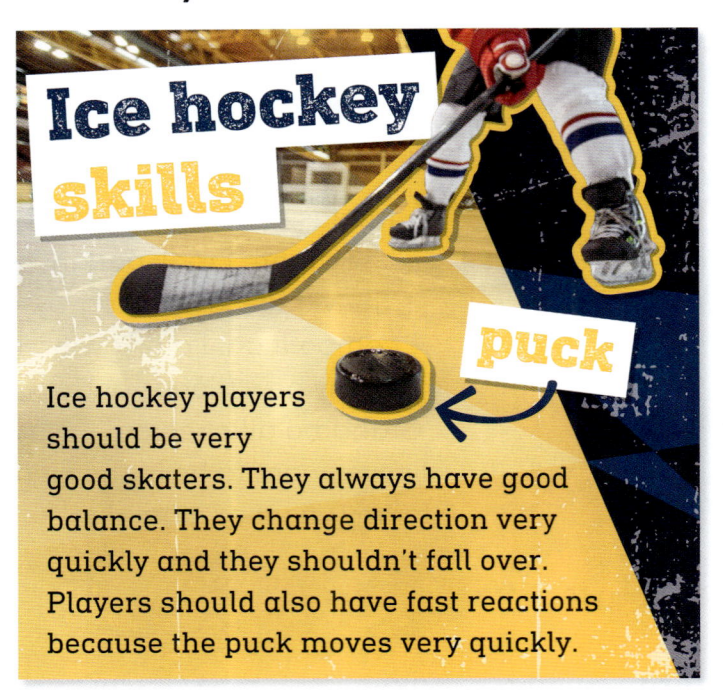

Ice hockey skills

puck

Ice hockey players should be very good skaters. They always have good balance. They change direction very quickly and they shouldn't fall over. Players should also have fast reactions because the puck moves very quickly.

2 Listen and complete.

arms   difficult   easy   eye   foot
hand   hits   kicks   puck   skate

Hand to _____ coordination

Ice hockey players have very good _____ to eye coordination. This means that they can hit the _____ when it is moving. They react quickly when they see the puck. They _____ towards it. They look at it, they move their _____ and hands, and the hockey stick _____ the puck. It's very _____ .

Watch a video about senses.

3 Read and complete.

ears   eyes   nose   skin   tongue

The five senses

When we see something, we are using one of our five senses. Our senses give us information. We see with our _____ . We hear with our _____ . Our _____ is in our mouth and we use it to taste food. We use our _____ to smell. _____ covers our body and we feel things with this using our hands and feet.

4 What senses do you need for ice hockey? Check ✓ and discuss.

hearing ☐   sight ☐   taste ☐
smell ☐   touch ☐

Hockey players use their sight when they hit the puck.

5 Choose a sport and ask and answer with a partner.

What senses do you use?   *How do you use them?*

96   ninety-six

EXPERIMENT TIME

What senses do I need for balancing?

	I think	Now I know
Sight	☐	☐
Hearing	☐	☐
Taste	☐	☐
Smell	☐	☐
Touch	☐	☐

Did you know?
A part of your inner ear is important for balance.

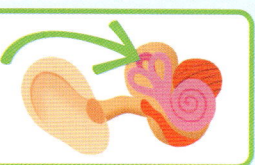

Materials
cushion   blindfold   stop watch

1. Take turns trying the balances.
2. How long can you balance for?
3. Time your friends and write the results in the table.

Names	Balance 1	Balance 2	Balance 3	Balance 4

Balance 1    Balance 2    Balance 3    Balance 4

6 Make a bar chart with the results for your group.

MATH ZONE
Choose a color for each friend.
Label the bars with the names in your group.

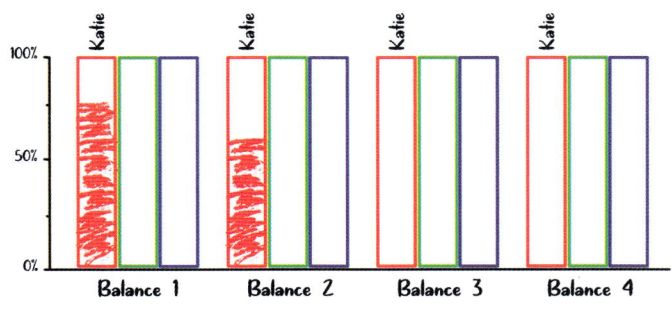

ninety-seven 97

Sharing out tasks
COMMUNICATION

*I will ask and answer using **should**.*

1 🎧 047 **Listen, look, and write the numbers.**

Maryam and her friends from the village are going to take part in a winter sports festival. They are going to do an ice-skating display. There is a list of tasks they should do before they go.

Should I make lunch for the journey?
Yes, that's a good idea.
Do you want me to invite other people?
No, it's OK, I can do that.

Maryam   Oliver   Nur   Adam

List of tasks
1. Organize the journey.
2. Make lunch for the journey.
3. Make name badges.
4. Clean ice skates.
5. Invite other people.
6. Practice every day.

2 💬 **Work with three friends and complete the list.**

Imagine you are going to take part in a festival.
1. Where are you going to go?
2. What are you going to do?
3. What should you do before you go?

List of tasks
Organize the journey.

3 💬 **Look at 2. Who will do the tasks? Ask and answer.**

Should I clean the equipment?

Yes!

Do you want me to make name badges?

Good idea!

98 ninety-eight

Writing lab
FLYERS

I will learn to write a flyer.

1 Read and complete. 7 to 17   clubs   exercising   friends   No   river   Oliver   Wednesday

ICE SKATING!

logo

COOL AS ICE
SKATE CLUB

- Do you like _____ ?
- Do you want to make new _____ ?
- Do you have good balance?

Come and join our skating club!
_____ experience needed.

WANTED! Active kids who like taking part in _____ .

Place: The boat house by the _____ .
Time: _____ and Saturday at 6 o'clock.
Contact: _____ at 650-555-3872.
Open for children and teenagers from _____ years old.

2 What is the flyer for? Read and check ✓.

1. It tells people about the ice-skating club.
2. It describes the movements in ice skating.
3. It explains good things about the ice-skating club.
4. It explains a skill for ice skating.
5. It is trying to sell something.
6. It gives information about the ice-skating club.

3 Check ✓ and complete.

Ice-skating club ☐   Choir ☐
Chess club ☐   Drama club ☐

Name of club: _____
Place you meet: _____
When you meet: _____
Name of contact: _____
Ages of club members: _____

4 Use your plan in **3** and make a flyer.

Don't forget to include …
1. … a logo.
2. … a skill people need.
3. … good things about the club.

ninety-nine 99

PROJECT AND REVIEW

Have a club fair

Step 1
Research

➤ Find out about types of clubs.

- ☐ Make a list of types of clubs.
- ☐ Ask your friends and find the favorite club.
- ☐ Think of activities the club can take part in.

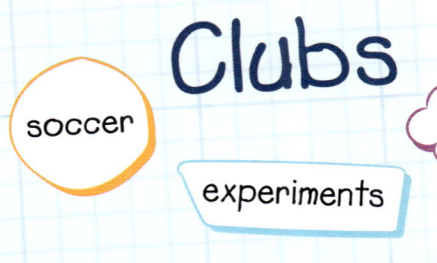

Clubs
- soccer
- chess
- experiments
- computer games
- choir

What's your favorite club?

I like computer games club.

We can invent a computer game and take part in a contest.

Step 2
Plan

➤ Invent a club logo and slogan.

- ☐ Choose a place and a time to meet.
- ☐ Invent rules and a slogan for the club.
- ☐ Decide on a logo for the club.
- ☐ What should and shouldn't you do at the club?
- ☐ What does the logo look like?

Rules
We should always share new ideas.
We should never post photos.

Slogans
share ideas
play new games

Place:
Time:

Step 3
Create

▸ Design a logo.

☐ Choose an item to put the logo on.
☐ Draw and color the logo on your item.
☐ Add the slogan to the logo.

share ideas,
play new games.

Tell your family about your club.

Step 4
Show and tell

▸ Present your club at the club fair.

☐ Set up a table for your club with the item you made.
☐ Present your club to your friends.
☐ Ask friends to join and write their names on a list.
☐ Find out which club is the favorite.

You should join our club because we always have new computer games. We invent our games. Sometimes we win computer game contests.

Now I can …

… use club activity words.

… talk about rules using *should*.

… ask and answer using *should*.

… write a flyer.

one hundred and one 101

3 Checkpoint
UNITS 5 AND 6

	Z always	G Z should	Z practice	never
G		Z	G more	G
	goes			
G Z get better	Z will	Z shouldn't		G fewer
	G doesn't practice	don't go	Z	G Z take part in
	G won't	G Z if		Z
sometimes	doesn't take part in	destroy	G be	Z G catch
G Z	Z meet	doesn't catch		make new friends

1 🎧 **Listen and write A in the squares.**

Antonio

2 Read and check ✓ the true sentences.

Z = Zoe
G = George

Zoe   George

1 Zoe should never practice skating. ☐
2 George should take part in more of the activities. ☐
3 If Zoe takes part in the activities, she will meet the tigers. ☐
4 If George doesn't practice chess, he won't make new friends. ☐
5 Zoe shouldn't catch the otters. ☐
6 If George catches the butterflies, there will be fewer. ☐

3 Complete the squares on the board. Then write a sentence.

☐ = actions
☐ = objects and places
☐ = other words

The children _____ never _____ _____ .

4 Write about yourself.

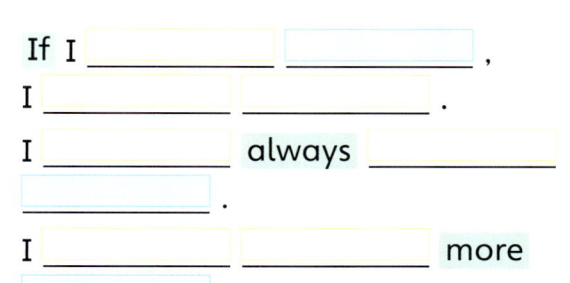

If I _____ _____ ,
I _____ _____ .
I _____ always _____ _____ .
I _____ _____ more _____ .

5 💬 Imagine you go to the wildlife camp. Ask and answer with a partner.

What will you do if you go to the wildlife camp?
— I will take part in the activities.

What will happen if you don't take part in the activities?
— I won't make new friends.

Should you catch the butterflies?
— No, you should never catch butterflies.

If you catch the butterflies, will there be fewer?
— Yes, there will.

one hundred and three   103

The Fathala Wildlife Reserve
CULTURE

1 Look and read. Underline the animals, plants, and the threats to both.

animals — plants
threats to animals
threats to plants

Senegal

Senegal is a country in North West Africa. There are deserts, grasslands, and forests. There are many wildlife centers and parks for protecting plants and animals.

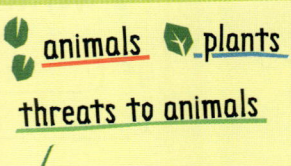

Fun Fact! Senegal has a man-made island made of shells!

The Fathala Wildlife Reserve in Senegal protects animals and plants. In the forest, there are lions, monkeys, giraffes, and zebras. In and around the rivers, there are crocodiles and many types of birds. The animals are threatened by loss of habitat and hunting.

The Baobab tree is the oldest type of tree in Africa. It stores water in its huge trunk. People eat the leaves and the seeds. The Baobab trees are under threat from climate change.

2 What do the animals say? Listen and match.

Awa   Issa

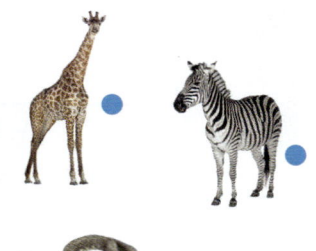

If we cut you down,

- … I won't have any oil for my skin.
- … I won't have a place to make my nest.
- … I won't have any leaves to eat.
- … I won't have any fruit to eat.

104   one hundred and four

3 Read and label the instruments.

Senegalese music and instruments

In Senegal, musicians get together to sing traditional stories about their history. Everybody joins in playing different instruments and singing. There are many different types of drums.

The djembe has a top part to play with your hands and a smaller bottom part to hold. The dundun is a large cylinder made from wood. The tama has strings around it that the musicians press and pull as they hit the drum with a stick. The musicians make the tama sound like somebody is talking.

Some musicians play a string instrument called the kora. It is like a guitar, but it has twenty-one strings. The musician plays eleven strings with the left hand and ten with the right hand.

My Culture

4 What music do you play in your culture? Discuss with a partner.

> In my culture, we play Mariachi music with a guitar!

5 Make and play a Senegalese drum.

Choose to make a tama drum or a djembe drum. Check ✓ a Senegalese animal to paint on your drum.

- lion ☐
- giraffe ☐
- zebra ☐
- snake ☐
- crocodile ☐

one hundred and five

7 Marvelous medicines

How can I make a plant fact file?

1 What do you think the building is? Why?

2 Listen and number in order.

- Claire likes to smell and touch the plants.
- Doctor Jones is in the sensory garden with Claire, Jojo, and Ismail.
- She can listen to the birds and insects.
- He likes to play in the water.
- Doctor Jones thinks the garden helps her patients get better.
- Ismail is at the hospital for a check-up and some new medicine.

3 What happened to Sarah? Read and complete the table with two checks ✓ for each person. Then listen and check.

CODE CRACKER

	Jack	Amy	Tom	Sarah	Ben
went to the hospital					
saw a doctor					
saw a nurse					
took medicine					
stayed in the hospital					

Jack and one of the girls went to the hospital. Jack and one of the girls saw a doctor. Two boys saw the nurse. One of them took medicine, but not Ben. Ben stayed in the hospital. One of the girls saw a doctor and took some medicine, but not Sarah.

4 A lot of medicines come from plants. Look at the images, what are they? Discuss with a partner.

one hundred and seven 107

What's the matter?
VOCABULARY

I will learn illness and medicine words.

1 🎧 052 **Listen and number. Sing the song.**

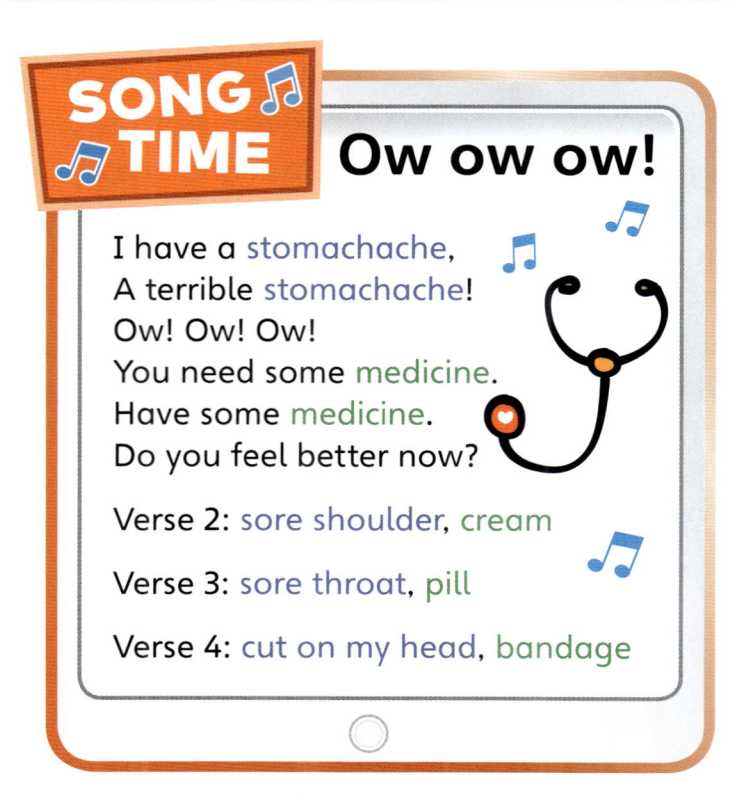

The nurse is going to give her patients a check-up.

SONG TIME 🎵 Ow ow ow!

I have a stomachache,
A terrible stomachache!
Ow! Ow! Ow!
You need some medicine.
Have some medicine.
Do you feel better now?

Verse 2: sore shoulder, cream

Verse 3: sore throat, pill

Verse 4: cut on my head, bandage

2 **Complete with words from the song and match to pictures.**

Look at the image and page 107 to help you.

1. Amy has a _____ .
   She needs a _____ .
2. Sara has a _____ .
   She needs some _____ .
3. Jack has a _____ .
   He needs some _____ .

3 💬 **Choose words and act out with a partner.**

… ache	sore …	cut on my …
ear	knee	leg
tooth	back	arm
back	neck	neck

What's the matter?

I have a backache.

108 one hundred and eight

4 Read and record Sam's temperature. Then answer the questions.

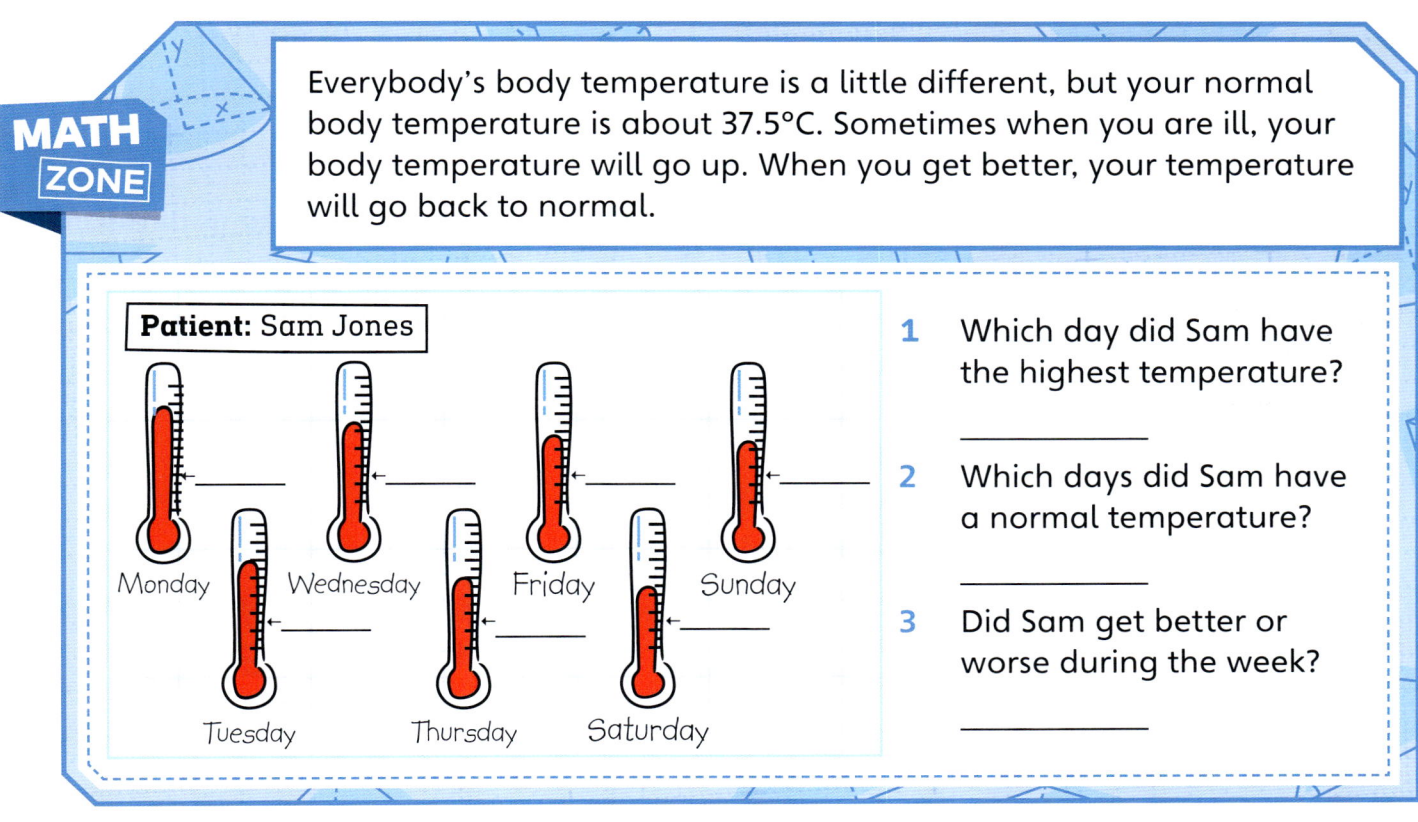

MATH ZONE

Everybody's body temperature is a little different, but your normal body temperature is about 37.5°C. Sometimes when you are ill, your body temperature will go up. When you get better, your temperature will go back to normal.

Patient: Sam Jones

Monday, Wednesday, Friday, Sunday
Tuesday, Thursday, Saturday

1. Which day did Sam have the highest temperature?
   _____
2. Which days did Sam have a normal temperature?
   _____
3. Did Sam get better or worse during the week?
   _____

5 Make your own picture dictionary. Label the body parts and things in a doctor's bag.

shoulder
thermometer

6 Listen and complete. Then say.

quarter   queen   questions   quickly   twelve   twenty   twins   twisted

Twenty _____ twisted their right foot. _____ twins _____ their left foot.

The quiet _____ _____ answered a _____ of the doctor's _____ .

1. How many feet are twisted?
   a twenty-two ☐
   b thirty-two ☐
   c sixty-four ☐

2. How many questions did she answer?
   a five ☐
   b ten ☐
   c fifteen ☐

7 Choose. Say it as quickly as you can.

one hundred and nine   109

Language lab
GRAMMAR: TO DO SOMETHING

I will learn to explain why we do something.

1 Watch the video.

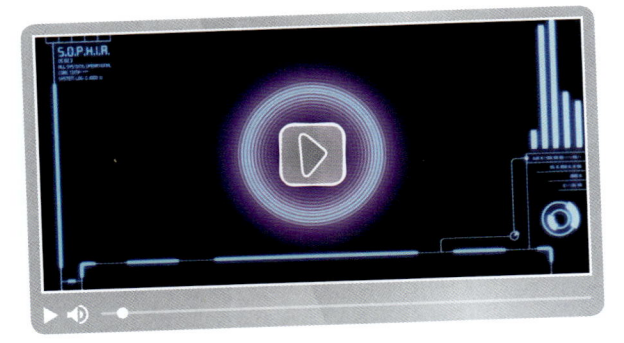

Doctors use medicine **to make** us better.
Dentists use X-rays **to see** our teeth.
Nurses use a thermometer **to take** our temperature.

2 Choose words to ask and answer with a partner.

How do doctors use _____ to make us better?

They use _____ …

… to _____ .

CODE CRACKER

bandages   cream   medicine   pills
thermometers   X-rays

bandages   cream   medicine   pills
thermometers   X-rays

back   bones   neck   stomach
temperature   throat

3 🎧 **Listen and match.**

Nurses use

Doctors use

Dentists use

thermometers   cream   medicine

pills   X-rays   water

- to see your teeth.
- to make you better.
- to stop headaches.
- to take your temperature.
- to clean your mouth.
- to put on sore skin.

4 💡 💬 **Check ✓ three things to give your friend who is ill. Then ask and answer with a partner.**

I'm going to bring a book.

Why?

To give my friend something to read.

5 🎨 **Make your friend a "Get well soon" card.**

Hi Sam,

I'm bringing you a lovely book to read in bed. I'm bringing you some delicious cookies to give you something nice to eat.

I hope you get well soon.

From, Angela

one hundred and eleven 111

Story lab
READING

I will read a story about a real event.

1 Look at the pictures. Is the story set in the past, present, or future?

Cholera outbreak!

One day, young Mary arrived at my house. "Please come quickly, Doctor. My father is very ill," she said. "What's the matter with him?" I asked. Mary told me that he had a terrible stomachache and a high temperature. I was very worried. I knew this was cholera and now nearly 300 people were dead. My patients needed to drink lots of water, but I didn't think the water was clean.

People collected water from pumps in the streets, but the streets were very dirty. I thought maybe the water was the problem. So I marked the water pumps on a map. When I visited a patient, I marked the house on the map, too. And then I saw a pattern. Most of the patients lived near the water pump on Broad Street.

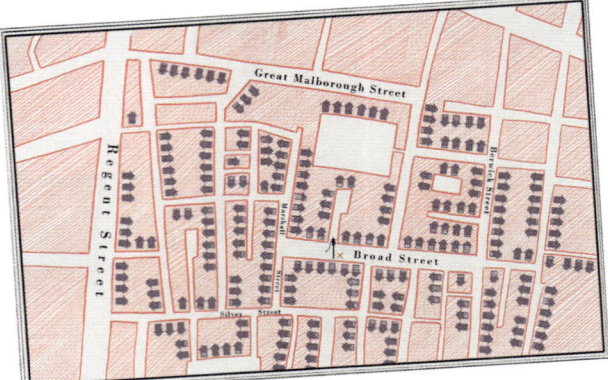

2 Read and listen.

3 Number the sentences in order. Which sentences happen before the story begins?

a. ☐ George's family moved to Broad Street.

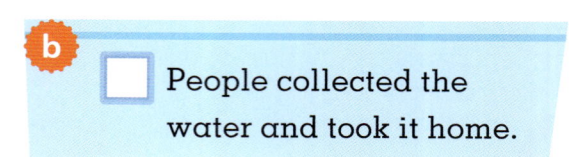

b. ☐ People collected the water and took it home.

c. ☐ Baby George got cholera.

d. ☐ The mother washed George's clothes at the water pump.

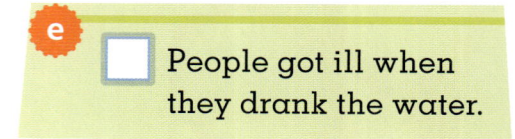

e. ☐ People got ill when they drank the water.

The next day, I took Harry, from the water company, to the pump to take off the handle so nobody could use it. Mary's mother wasn't happy! "How am I going to get water now?" she asked angrily. Harry told her to use the water pump on Carnaby Street.

After a week, fewer people were ill, but there was a baby on Broad Street that had cholera. I asked his mother if she gave the baby water from the pump on Broad Street. "No," she said. Then she told me that her baby was ill before she came to Broad Street. "Did you wash your baby's clothes at the water pump?" I asked. "Yes, my George is always very clean!" she exclaimed.

Now I understood! The baby's dirty clothes polluted the water that people collected at the pump and took the cholera back to their houses. That's how the illness traveled! I told Harry to put up notices near all the pumps. Soon the cholera outbreak was over and everybody was very careful to keep the drinking water clean.

Values Care for yourself.

4 Read and complete with should or shouldn't.

1. You _____ call a doctor if you are ill.
2. You _____ drink dirty water.
3. You _____ wash dirty clothes near the water pump.
4. You _____ stay at home if you are ill.

5 How did Dr. Snow stop the cholera outbreak? Answer the questions.

1. What was the problem?
   _____
2. What research did he do?
   _____
3. What did he notice?
   _____
4. What was his solution?
   _____
5. What happened next?
   _____

6 Act out the story in groups.

Experiment lab
SCIENCE: TRACKING GERMS

I will learn how to track germs.

1 🦠 **Listen and number the bacteria.** ▶ **Watch a video about bacteria.**

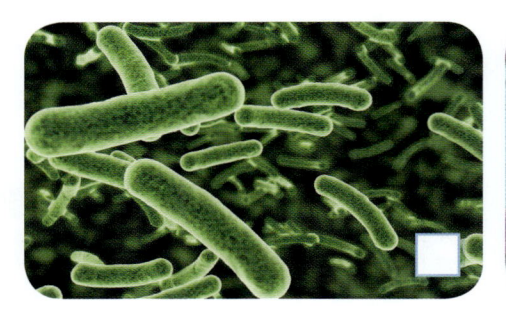

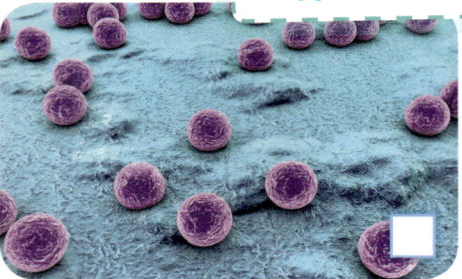

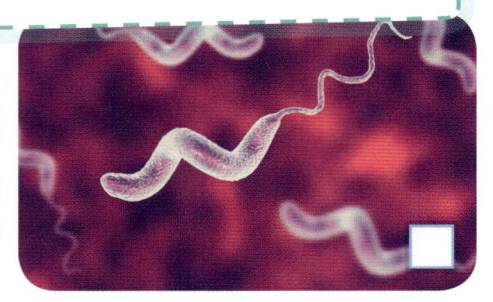

2 🦠 **Read, listen, and answer.**

Bacteria are germs. Doctors use microscopes to find out the germs that are making people ill. Then they choose the best medicine to help them get better. Germs can live everywhere. They can live on food, in water, in and on our bodies, and even in outer space! Not all germs are harmful. We have bacteria in our stomach that help us to digest food. We use bacteria, like penicillin, to make medicines.

1 How can we see them? _____
2 Why are they dangerous? _____
3 What do doctors do to help us? _____
4 Where do they live? _____
5 Why are they helpful? _____

3 💡 **Complete with before and after.**

Germs can travel through touch.
It is important to wash your hands:

1 _____ you sneeze or cough.
2 _____ you touch or eat food.
3 _____ you play with dirt.
4 _____ you use the bathroom.
5 _____ you touch a pet.

4. What should you do to stop germs? Discuss with a partner.

You should cover your nose when you sneeze.

You shouldn't share a tooth brush with your friend.

EXPERIMENT TIME

How do you track germs?

1. Break the chalk into small pieces on the plates and crush them into a powder with the back of the spoon.
2. Two students cover their hands in blue or red chalk.
3. Continue with your class.
4. At the end of the class look to see where there are blue and red chalk marks. The marks show where the students left their germs.
5. Complete the table and sentences.

Materials

1 red chalk stick   1 blue chalk stick
A spoon   2 plates   A light

Germ tracker	Red germs	Blue germs
How many people have the germs on their hands?		
How many people have the germs on their clothes?		
How many people have the germs on their faces?		
Where else did you find the germs?		

We found red germs on _____.
We found blue germs on _____.
In our classroom the _____ germs traveled more than the _____ germs.

My head hurts!
COMMUNICATION

I will ask and answer about illnesses.

My head **hurts**.
I have a **headache**.
Her stomach **doesn't hurt**.
She doesn't have a **stomachache**.
Does your ear **hurt**?
Do you have an **earache**?

1 Read and match.

- What's the matter, Alex?
- Do you have a temperature?
- Does your neck hurt?
- Here's some medicine.

- I have a headache.
- Yes, it's sore.
- Thank you, Doctor Khan.
- I think so.

2 Look at the key and complete.

1 _____ : What's the matter?
1 _____ : I have 2 _____ .
1 _____ : Then go to the 3 _____ .
3 _____ : Hello! What's the matter?
1 _____ : I have a terrible 2 _____ .
3 _____ : Does your 4 _____ hurt?
1 _____ : 5 _____ .
3 _____ : Here's 6 _____ .

CODE CRACKER

1 = person (me, Mom, …)
2 = problem (…ache)
3 = doctor, nurse, dentist
4 = parts of the body
5 = yes/no …
6 = solution (cream, medicine, pills, bandage)

3 Look at 2 and act out with a partner.

Writing lab
DOCTOR'S REPORT

I will learn to write a simple doctor's report.

1 How long was the patient ill? Read, answer, and complete.

check-up   earache   medicine   neck   temperature   X-ray

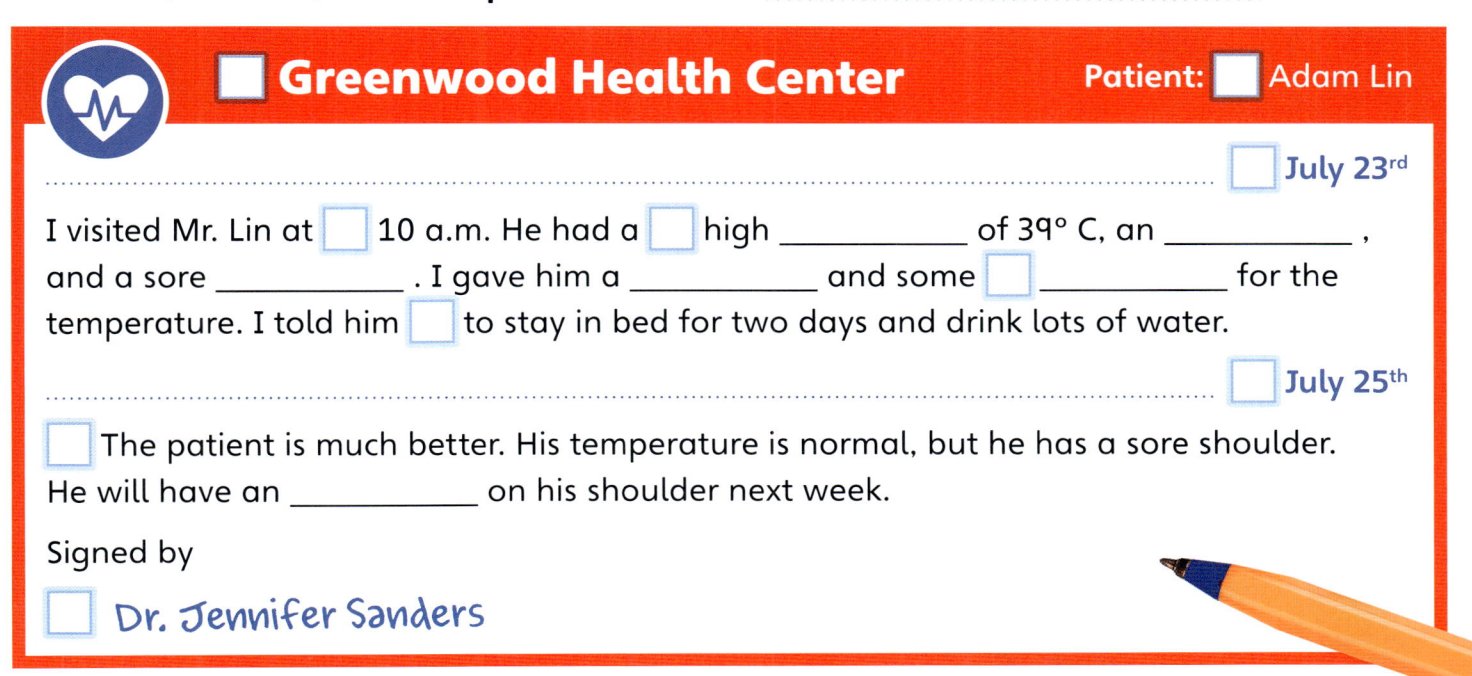

Greenwood Health Center   Patient: Adam Lin

July 23rd

I visited Mr. Lin at 10 a.m. He had a high _____ of 39° C, an _____, and a sore _____. I gave him a _____ and some _____ for the temperature. I told him to stay in bed for two days and drink lots of water.

July 25th

The patient is much better. His temperature is normal, but he has a sore shoulder. He will have an _____ on his shoulder next week.

Signed by

Dr. Jennifer Sanders

---

2 Number the features in **1**.

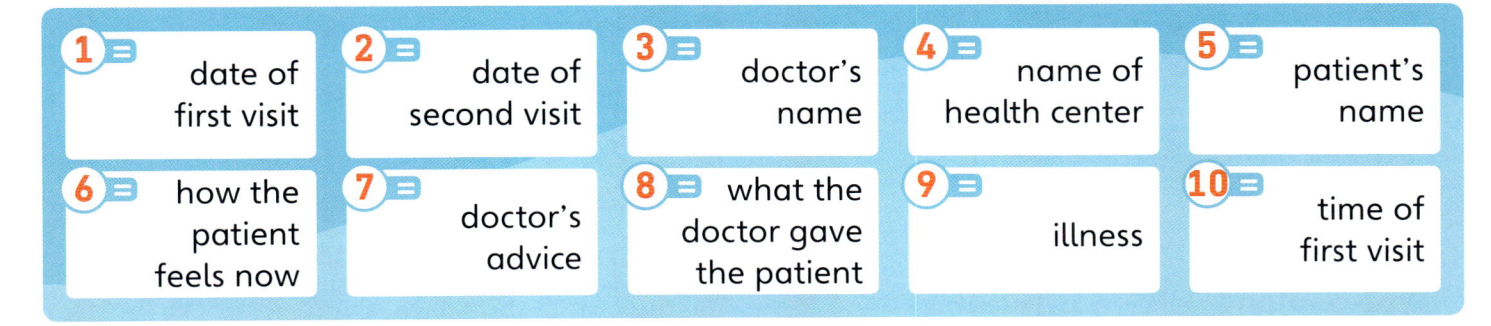

1. date of first visit
2. date of second visit
3. doctor's name
4. name of health center
5. patient's name
6. how the patient feels now
7. doctor's advice
8. what the doctor gave the patient
9. illness
10. time of first visit

3 What are the problems and solutions? Discuss with a partner.

bandage   cream   headache   medicine   pills   sore knee   sore shoulder   stomachache   temperature   toothache   X-ray

A sore knee is a problem.

I agree. Pills and a bandage is a solution.

4 Use the words in **3** and write a doctor's report.

one hundred and seventeen 117

PROJECT AND REVIEW

Make a plant fact file

Step 1

Research

> Find out about plants used for medicines.

- ☐ Find out about plants and the medicines they make.
- ☐ Research the illnesses that medicine helps.
- ☐ Make a chart with the information you find.

Plants	
	 foxglove
Illness used for	heart illnesses
Type of plant	tall purple flowers
Where it grows	in sunny gardens
Part used	the leaves

Step 2

Plan

> Plan how to make your fact file.

- ☐ Make a list of the materials you will need.
- ☐ Choose one of the plants from your table.
- ☐ Find a picture of your plant.

Materials

paper
pencil
coloring pencils
crayons
colored paints
picture of my plant

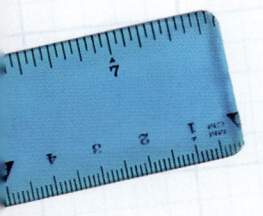

Step 3

Create

> Draw your plant and write your facts.

- ☐ Draw and color in your plant.
- ☐ Write about your plant.
- ☐ Put the facts from the class together to make a fact file.

Drawing plants
1. Trace the outline of the plant and copy onto paper.
2. Look very carefully at the picture.
3. Draw the details of the plant.
4. Color in your drawing.

The willow tree

People used willow bark to make medicine that helps people when they have a high temperature. It makes their temperatures go down to normal. Today, we still use the same plant.

Tell your family about your plant fact file. Then ask them about plants they used for medicine.

Step 4

Show and tell

> Present your fact file.

- ☐ Present your fact file.
- ☐ Ask your friends questions about the information you gave them.
- ☐ Find who chose the same plant.
- ☐ Compare your drawings and information.

"Willow trees grow near water."

Now I can …

- … use illness and medicine words.
- … explain why we do something.
- … ask and answer about illnesses.
- … write a doctor's report.

one hundred and nineteen 119

8 Theme parks

How can I make a model theme park ride?

1 💡 Do you like the rides? Are they dangerous?

2 Read and complete.

Rides   Food

_____   _____
_____   _____

A DAY OUT FOR ALL THE FAMILY!

Theme parks can be about nature, history, or the movies, but they always have lots of rides and attractions. You can ride on a **Ferris wheel** and a **roller coaster**. There are restaurants and cafés, and there are lots of food stalls. If you are hungry, you can buy **popcorn** or ice cream.

3 What is your favorite theme for a theme park? Decide on four with a partner.

4 Write a survey with your themes in **3**. Then ask and answer with friends.

Names	Favorite themes			

What is your favorite theme from my list?

I like the animal theme best.

Why?

Because I like pandas and dolphins!

one hundred and twenty-one   121

Rides!
VOCABULARY

I will learn theme park words.

1 🎧 058 **Listen and number. Sing the song.**

Ferris wheel ☐

bumper car ☐

roller coaster ☐

2 💡 **Complete the answers.**

What do you do before a ride starts?

What do you do when the ride starts?

How do you feel on the ride?

First, I _____ . Then I _____ .
When I am on the ride, I _____ .
I feel _____ and _____ !

3 💬 **Check ✓ two snacks you want. Then ask two friends and complete.**

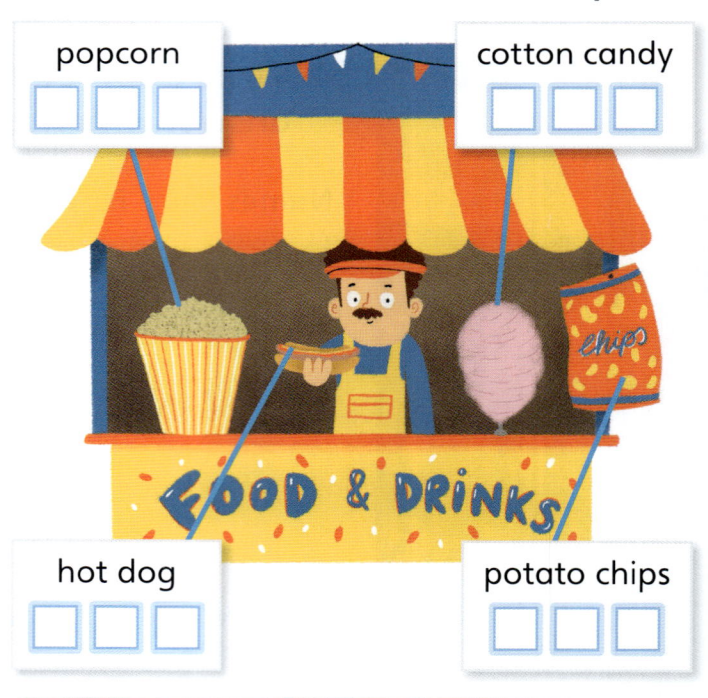

popcorn ☐☐☐

cotton candy ☐☐☐

hot dog ☐☐☐

potato chips ☐☐☐

What snacks would you like, Katie?

I'd like some cotton candy and a hot dog, please.

SONG TIME 🎵

Take a seat

Let's ride the …
Are you **interested**? Are you **worried**?
Come and **stand in line**.
Now **take a seat** on the …
Are you **excited**? Are you **scared**?
Let's **scream**!

one hundred and twenty-two

4 Can you buy your friends snacks? Look and complete.

MATH ZONE

COTTON CANDY	1 token		SPECIAL OFFER!!	3 hot dogs for 6 tokens
POPCORN			POTATO CHIPS	
big bag	3 tokens		big bag	2 tokens
small bag	2 tokens		small bag	1 token
HOT DOG	3 tokens			

You have 15 tokens. Look at your friends' favorite snacks in **3**. Can you buy all of the snacks? Add up the tokens.
Do you have any extra tokens?

Snacks: _____   Cost: _____   Snacks: _____   Cost: _____

Snacks: _____   Cost: _____   Snacks: _____   Cost: _____

Total Cost: _____   I have _____ extra tokens.

5 Make your own picture dictionary. Draw and write the words in four groups: *Actions, Food, Feelings,* and *Rides*.

Actions: stand in line
Food: popcorn
Feelings: excited
Rides: Ferris wheel

6 Ph 059 ▶ Listen and circle. Then say.

1. The space / ice race starts in the center of the city of space / ice .
2. The huge jelly / giant has orange jelly / giants on his jacket.

7 Ph ▶ Choose. Say it as quickly as you can.

Language lab
GRAMMAR: PAST, PRESENT, AND FUTURE

I will learn to compare the past, present, and future.

1 Watch the video.

> She **went** to the dinosaur race.
> She **is looking at** the fossil exhibition.
> She **will go** on the roller coaster.

2 Listen and complete.

Anna

David

DINO PARK — RIDES AND ATTRACTIONS

	Times
Dinosaur Race	_____
T-Rex roller coaster	_____
Fossil exhibition	_____
Bumper cars	_____
Ferris wheel	_____
Gymnastics show	_____

3 Look at 2. Read and complete.

1. Anna went to the dinosaur race at 11:30. She'll go to the fossil exhibition at 1:00. What is she doing now?

   She's _____
   _____ .

2. David went on the bumper cars at 2:30. He'll go to the gymnastics exhibition at 3:30. What is he doing now?

   He's _____
   _____ .

4 Choose a ride or attraction and make a token.

> Dino token for ... a ride on the bumper cars!

5 Can you use your token? Choose a clock and answer. Then complete.

11:30   **1:30**   **2:30**

This is for the T-Rex roller coaster.

No, I can't. They went at twelve thirty.

Yes, I can. They'll go at twelve thirty.

It's 1:30. Can you go with Anna and David?

It's 11:30. Can you go with Anna and David?

can   can't   didn't go   went   will go   won't go

1 I _____ go _____ with Anna and David because they _____ in ___ hour(s).

2 I _____ go _____ with Anna and David because they _____ _____ hour(s) ago.

6 Plan a day at Dino Park. Then play *Guess the ride or attraction* with a partner.

RIDES AND ATTRACTIONS

DINO PARK

	Times		Times
Dinosaur Race	_____	Bumper cars	_____
T-Rex roller coaster	_____	Ferris wheel	_____
Fossil exhibition	_____	Gymnastics show	_____

Story lab
REDAING

I will read a story about a theme park adventure.

1 Look at the pictures. Who or what is lost?

2 Read and listen.

Who's lost?

1 Yong and Meili were very excited about their visit to the theme park. First, they went on the roller coaster.

2 Then Uncle Bohai bought an ice cream for Yong and some popcorn for Meili. They were sitting at an outdoor café, when Meili shouted. "Look! There's my friend, Yuyan!" At the same moment, there was an announcement.

Suddenly lots and lots of people were standing up and running around.

3 Five minutes later, the café was empty.

The gymnastics display will start in five minutes.

Where's your sister?

Look! There's some popcorn on the floor.

3 Complete the sentences.

brother   friend   sister   uncle

1 Meili is Yong's _____ .
2 Bohai is Yong's _____ .
3 Yong is Meili's _____ .
4 Yuyan is Meili's _____ .

4 At the gymnastics display, Yong heard a scream.

They pushed through people but they didn't find Meili.

5 "Maybe she's riding the bumper cars." Uncle Bohai said. They stood in line and looked around. But she wasn't there. When they left the bumper cars, they sat down on a bench and Yong started to cry.

And then Yong saw Meili's hat on the ground. It was in front of an information office. He ran towards the office.

6 Meili was with her friend Yuyan, and Yuyan's family. "I was looking all over the park for you!" she said. "You were lost!"

Over here!

I can hear her, Uncle Bohai!

I'm a terrible uncle!

Where's my little sister? I'm scared!

Where were you?

Where were you?

Values Be responsible.

4 Answer the questions.

1. Where does Uncle Bohai lose Meili?
2. Why does he lose her?
3. What clue does Yong see first? Is it a good clue?
4. Where does Yong hear Meili? Does he see her?
5. What clue does Yong see next? Is it a good clue?
6. Who is Meili with?
7. Why does Meili think Yong was lost?

5 Who made the mistakes? Read and write the names.

Uncle Bohai, Yong, and Meili all made mistakes at the park.

1. Someone didn't ask permission. _____
2. Someone didn't watch the children. _____
3. Someone didn't go to the information office at once. _____
4. Someone didn't stay in the same place. _____

6 Act out the story in groups.

one hundred and twenty-seven 127

Experiment lab
SCIENCE: FORCES OF MOTION

I will learn how to test friction on a slide.

1 Read, listen, and color the arrows. ▶ Watch a video about friction.

How does a roller coaster work?

A roller coaster starts at the top of a hill. It falls to the bottom of the hill because of gravity. Roller coasters fall faster when the hill is higher.

When the roller coaster gets to the bottom, it starts to go up the next hill. It slows down because of gravity, but it doesn't stop because it has some momentum, or energy, from the fall. When the roller coaster gets to the top of the next hill, the same thing happens again.

When the roller coaster goes up and down the hills, it rubs against the slide. This slows down the movement. We call this *friction*. Friction always happens when two objects rub against each other.

➡ = momentum
➡ = gravity
➡ = friction

2 Read, listen, and number in order.

How does a spinner work?

When a spinner turns, the movement pushes objects inside the spinner away from the center. We call this a *centrifugal force*. It makes objects travel in a straight line outwards. The wall of the spinner stops the objects, but the centrifugal force is still pushing. The result is the objects stay in the same place. If there are holes in the wall, a small object will continue moving in a straight line.

a   b    c

128 one hundred and twenty-eight

3 What forces of motion do these rides have? Discuss with a partner.

The spinner has a centrifugal force.

Ferris wheel · spinner · roller coaster

4 Check ✓ the variables for the experiment.

- length of the slide ☐
- size of the marble ☐
- sounds ☐
- surface of the slide ☐
- temperature ☐

Variable = something that can change the results of an experiment.

marble · slide

EXPERIMENT TIME

How can I test friction on a slide?

Materials
- 1 meter ruler
- 3 blocks
- 1 small marble
- aluminum foil
- liquid glue
- sugar
- a stop watch

	1	2
Roll 1		
Roll 2		
Roll 3		

Experiment 1
1. Cover the ruler with aluminum foil.
2. Make a slide with the ruler and the blocks.
3. Roll the marble down the slide. Make a note of the time. Repeat three times.

Experiment 2
1. Cover the aluminum foil with glue and sugar.
2. Cover the marble in glue and sugar.
3. Roll the marble down the slide. Make a note of the time. Repeat three times.

faster   less   more   slower

In Experiment 1, the marble goes _____ because the surface has _____ friction.

In Experiment 2, the marble goes _____ because the surface has _____ friction.

one hundred and twenty-nine 129

Expressing feelings
COMMUNICATION

I will express my feelings.

1 🎧 064 **Listen and complete.**

animals   pandas   roller coaster   time

Yong   Meili   Bohai

1 What is Uncle Bohai worried about?
He's worried about the _____ .

2 What are Meili and Uncle Bohai scared of?
They are scared of the _____ .

4 What are Yong and Meili interested in?
They are interested in _____ .

5 What is Yong excited about?
He's excited about the _____ .

2 💬 **How do you feel about rides and attractions? Discuss with a partner.**

excited about   interested in
scared of   worried about

exhibitions   Ferris wheel   long line
roller coaster   snacks   spinner

What are you interested in?

I'm interested in the exhibitions.

I'm **scared of** roller coasters.
I'm **interested in** dinosaurs.
I'm **worried about** the long line for the Ferris wheel.
I'm **excited about** the new attractions.

3 Use words from 2. What ride or attraction does your group want to try?

CODE CRACKER

Yes! I'm ②①!
So am I!
How about going on the ①?
Me, too!
Oh, no! I'm ②①!
What about the ①?

The ride or attraction our group wants to try is the _____ .

① = theme park ride or attraction
② = feelings

130 one hundred and thirty

Writing lab
LOST PROPERTY FORM

I will learn to fill out a lost property form.

1 Read and complete. Then underline the words.

> 745-555-9219   Beach Street   café   green hat
> gymnastics display   June 15th   Ocean   roller coaster

_____ THEME PARK

LOST PROPERTY FORM

Name: Li Meili
Address: 115 _____

Information about a person _____
Information about time _____
Information about the day at the park _____

Telephone number: _____
Lost Object: A _____ with yellow flowers.
Date: Saturday, _____
Time of day: the morning
Last place you had the object: I had my hat at the _____.

Other notes:
I saw the _____
_____
and I went on the _____
_____.

2 Imagine you lost something. Ask and answer with a partner.

- What did you lose? — I lost my keys.
- Where were you? — I think I was on the bumper cars.
- What did you do next? — I went to a café.

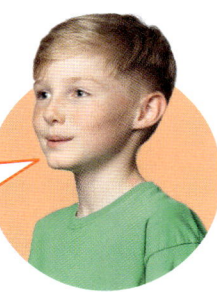

3 Make a lost property form. Then swap with your partner to complete.

PROJECT AND REVIEW

Make a model theme park ride

Step 1

Research

> Find out about different types of theme parks.

- [ ] Make a list of theme parks in your country.
- [ ] Research different types of rides.
- [ ] Find the differences between the theme parks.

Theme parks
Ocean View   Movie World   Space Park

"All the theme parks have roller coasters."

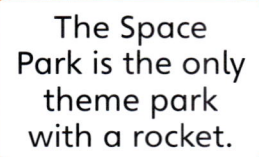

"The Space Park is the only theme park with a rocket."

Step 2

Plan

> Plan the materials you will use.

- [ ] In groups, choose a name and a theme for your park.
- [ ] In pairs, choose a ride to make.
- [ ] Identify ride pieces you need.
- [ ] Collect materials you need.

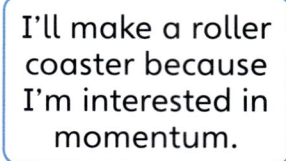

"I'll make a roller coaster because I'm interested in momentum."

132   one hundred and thirty-two

Step 3
Create

> Make a model theme park ride.

- ☐ Make your ride from recycled materials.
- ☐ Give the ride a name and make a sign.
- ☐ In groups, make a board for your theme park.
- ☐ Follow the theme and decorate your ride and the board.

Tell your family how you made the ride. Ask them how they feel about theme parks.

Step 4
Show and tell

> Present your theme park.

- ☐ Explain the name of your theme park.
- ☐ Describe the materials you used to make the rides.
- ☐ Guess the ride from the materials that were used.

This theme park is about transportation because Maryam is interested in trains.

I used a plastic container to make my ride.

Those are the bumper cars!

Now I can ...

- ... use theme park words.
- ... compare the past, present, and future.
- ... express my feelings.
- ... fill in a lost property form.

one hundred and thirty-three 133

4 Checkpoint
UNITS 7 AND 8

G (Ferris wheel)	yesterday	A took	rode	to buy
(roller coaster)	A (pills)	(toothpaste)	in the afternoon	A (doctor)
had	G isn't going to ride	G is going to buy	A (itchy face)	G A in the morning
(tickets)	A went	A (headache)	G (cotton candy)	A didn't have
(stomachache boy)	stood in line	A at night	to make her better	(hot dog)
G (popcorn)	used / didn't use	A to get	didn't go	G tomorrow
(potato chips)	didn't have a go	G isn't going to stand in line	(cough syrup)	is going to ride
(thermometer)				

1 🎧 065 **Listen and write Z in the squares.**

Zoe

2 Read and check ✓ the true sentences.

G = George
A = Antonio

Antonio   George

1 Antonio had a temperature at night. ☐
2 He went to the doctor to get some medicine. ☐
3 He didn't have a headache in the morning. ☐
4 George is going to stand in line for popcorn tomorrow. ☐
5 He isn't going to ride the Ferris wheel. ☐
6 He's going to buy a hot dog in the morning. ☐

3 Complete the squares on the board. Write one sentence.

☐ = actions and reasons
☐ = objects
☐ = times

George _____
_____ to _____ _____.

4 Write about yourself.

_____ I _____ _____ to
_____ _____.
I _____ _____ _____.
I _____ _____ _____.

5 💬 Ask and answer with a partner.

Why did you go to the doctor yesterday?
— I went to get some medicine.

Why?
— Because I had a stomachache.

What are you going to do tomorrow?
— I'm going to ride the roller coaster.

Are you going to stand in line?
— Yes, I think so.

Test your progress with English Benchmark Young Learners

one hundred and thirty-five 135

Fairgrounds and The Goose Fair
CULTURE

1 How are the children's lives different from yours? Read and discuss.

In England, during the summer months, fairgrounds open all over the country. The first fair every year is on February 14th, in a town called King's Lynn. The last fair every year is on November 15th, in a town called Loughborough. These two fairs are more than 800 years old. Between February and November there are fairs every weekend at different places in England. Some children travel and work with their parents at these fairs.

The United Kingdom

The United Kingdom is made up of England, Scotland, Wales, and Northern Ireland. People from many different cultures live in the UK.

Fun Fact!
The river Thames in London, England has over 200 bridges!

2 Listen and check ✓ the true sentences.

1. Ella hurt her arm helping her father with the roller coaster.
2. James likes going to school.
3. Ella wants to be a doctor.
4. James doesn't want to work in the fairground.
5. Both children will help at the fairground this summer.

3 Listen again. What jobs will the children do? Complete the sentences.

Ella wants to be a _____ . She will _____ .

James wants to be a _____ .
He will _____ .

4 **Read and answer.**

The Goose Fair is one of England's most famous fairs. It takes place in Nottinghamshire and is over 700 years old. Historians think it's called The Goose Fair because farmers used to go to the market square to sell geese. The same market square is where the fair started.

Now the fair has more than 500 "attractions" or rides like bumper cars, rollercoasters, ghost trains, and helter skelter slides. It sells traditional fun fair food like cotton candy and donuts but also international food like churros! There is something for everyone at The Goose Fair.

1 Are historians 100% sure why it's called The Goose Fair? Why do they think it is?
   _____

2 What attractions are at The Goose Fair?
   _____

3 What can you eat in The Goose Fair?
   _____

My Culture

5 **Make a traveling fun kit.**

Choose two games and follow the instructions to make your fun kit.

Have you got two of these?

No!

Is it in your neck?

Yes!

one hundred and thirty-seven   137

Wordlist

Welcome Unit

Family Vocabulary
aunt
grandparents
parents
uncle

Ordinal Numbers
1st–31st

Unit 1

In the Forest/ Survival Vocabulary
blanket
boots
branches
compass
gloves
grass
leaves
map
matches
rope
wheel
whistle

Phonics
bird
fir
girl
heard
shirt
skirt

Experiment lab
arch bridge
deck
force
pentagon
pull up
push down
structure
suspension bridge
triangle
truss bridge

Unit 2

Into The Past Vocabulary
ate
beans
built
cocoa
drank
grew
jewelry
made
maize
pyramid
turkey
wore

Phonics
bear
chair
fair
hair
square
there
wears

Experiment lab
ancient
Arabic numbers
Chinese
Egyptian
Mayan
number square
number system

Culture lab
duodji
Finland
flag
friendship bracelet
reindeer
Saami

Unit 3

Space Vocabulary
control panel
Earth
engine
fuel
gravity
handle
lights
oxygen
planet
radio
screen
seat

Phonics
clear
hears
near
nearly
really
year

Experiment lab
distances
echo
louder
quieter
sound
source
vibrate
waves

Unit 4

Dragons Vocabulary
brave
burn
dangerous
east
fly
north
sleep
strong
village
west

Phonics
blanket
blue
clean
clocks
clouds
flies
floor
flowers
glass
places
plates
sleeps

Experiment lab
air resistance
bi-plane
engine
jet plane
lift
propeller
pull
push
streamlined
weight
wheels
windows
wings

Culture lab
coral reef
eco house
fishing boat
Guna Yala
island
lunar eclipse
moon
Panama

Unit 5

Endangered Animals Vocabulary
butterfly
chemicals
eagle
field
habitat
mountain
otter
pollution
threat
tiger
turtle
wolf

Phonics
bridge
brown
crab
cranky
dragon
dreamy
friendly
frog
grass
gray
green
grouse
growing
princess
prissy
tree
triangular

Experiment lab
2D
3D
depth
height
light box
negative shapes
positive shapes
sides
width

Wordlist

Unit 6

Join In! Vocabulary
cheer
chess
choir
contest
drama
get better
ice-skating
make new friends
meet
neighborhood
practice
take part in

Phonics
school
score
skating
smallest
smiling
snails
snow
spaces
Spain
special
stand
start
stop
swan
sweet

Experiment lab
change direction
coordination
fast reactions
good balance
hearing
ice hockey
puck
senses
sight
skin
smell
taste
tongue
touch

Culture lab
Africa
Baobab tree
crocodiles
djembe drum
dundun drum
giraffes
kora
lions
monkeys
Senegal
tama drum
wildlife reserve
zebras

Unit 7

Marvelous Medicine Vocabulary
bandage
check-up
cream
medicine
neck
patient
pill
sore shoulder
sore throat
stomachache
temperature
thermometer

Phonics
quarter
queen
questions
quickly
quiet
twelve
twenty
twins
twisted

Experiment lab
bacteria
cough
germs
microscope
sneeze

Unit 8
Theme Park Vocabulary
bumper cars
cotton candy
excited
Ferris wheel
hot dogs
interested
popcorn
potato chips
roller coaster
scared
scream
spinner
stand in line
take your seat
worried

Phonics
center
city
giant
huge
ice
jacket
jelly
orange
race
space

Experiment lab
centrifugal force
friction
gravity
momentum
movement
slide
variable

Culture lab
churros
donuts
fair
fairground
farmers
geese
summer
the United Kingdom
winter

Continents
Africa
Antarctica
Asia
Australia
Europe
North America
South America

Grammar Reference
LEVEL 3 REVISION

Unit 1

Language lab 1

Present Progressive:

What *are you doing*?
I'm riding the bus with my friends.
We're going to school.

What*'s* he *doing*?
He's drawing. *He isn't reading*.

What *are they doing*?
They're singing. *They aren't acting*.

Is she waving?
Yes, *she is*.

Are they drinking juice?
No, *they aren't*.

Language lab 2

Present Progressive with adverbs of manner:

I'm juggling *well*.
He's drawing *beautifully*.
They're singing *badly*.
We're going to school *quickly*.
We're not going to school *slowly*.

Unit 2

Language lab 1

Simple Past of *be*:

It *was* snowy last winter.
It *wasn't* warm.
We *were* in the yard.

Was it windy?
Yes, it *was*.

Were you tired?
No, we *weren't*.

Language lab 2

There was / There were:

There was a tree in the yard. *There wasn't* a path.
There were birds in the yard. *There weren't* any rabbits.

Was there a cat?
No, *there wasn't*.
Were there nuts on the table? Yes, *there were*.

Unit 3

Language lab 1

Comparatives:

The show is *more exciting* than the play.
The show is *noisier* than the play.
The play is *quieter* than the show.
The music at the play is *worse* than the music at the show.

Language lab 2

Superlatives:

This is the *best* show ever!
It has the *biggest* and the *most colorful* stage in the world.
The magic tricks are the *most exciting* part of the show.
The people on stage wear the *funniest* clothes, but the music is the *worst* I've ever heard.

Unit 4

Language lab 1

Simple Past with regular verbs:

I *traveled* by train.
I *didn't travel* by airplane.
You *visited* your aunty.
You *didn't visit* your uncle.
He *studied* math yesterday.
He *didn't study* English.
She *worked* in the farm.
She *didn't work* in the cafe.
They *played* soccer.
They *didn't play* basketball.

Language lab 2

Simple Past with regular verbs:

Where *did* you *travel* to?
I *traveled* to Mexico.

When *did* she *work* at the bakery?
She *worked* there on Saturday.

Who *did* he *study* with?
He *studied* with his friend.

Did you *swim* in the river?
No, I *didn't*.

Did she *walk* to the store?
Yes, she *did*.

one hundred and forty three 143

Grammar Reference
LEVEL 3 REVISION

Unit 5

Language lab 1
Simple Past with irregular verbs:

I *went* to the cafe and I *bought* some juice.
You *did* your homework.
He *sat* on the chair. He *didn't sit* on the table.
She *saw* her friend. She *didn't see* her teacher.
We *had* three pencils. We *didn't have* an eraser.
They *ate* all the cookies.
They *didn't eat* all the salad.

Language lab 2
Simple Past with irregular verbs:

Did you *buy* some water?
No, I *didn't*.

Where *did* she *do* her homework?
She *did* her homework in the library.

How many pencils *did* they *have*?
They *had* three pencils.

What *did* they *eat*?
They *ate* cookies.

Unit 6

Language lab 1
Countable and uncountable nouns:

There is *a* kite in the toy store.
There is *an* astronaut in the toy store.
There is *some* bread in the bakery.
There are *some* cakes in the cafe.
There isn't *any* cheese in the market.

Language lab 2
Countable and uncountable nouns:

There's *a lot of* bread in the bakery.
There are *lots of* balls in the toy store.
There isn't *much* pizza left.
There aren't *many* cookies in the jar.

How *much* money does the kite cost? $10
How *many* cakes are there? There are three cakes.

Unit 7

Language lab 1

Going to to talk about the future:

What are you *going to* do tomorrow?
I'm *going to* go to the beach with my family.
Mom's *going to* relax. She *isn't going to* cook.
My brothers are *going to* go surfing.
I'm *not going to* go surfing.

Language lab 2

Infinitives of purpose: want to and would like to:

I *want to* go on a boat trip. I *'d like to* see a dolphin. I *don't want to* see a shark. I *wouldn't like to* see its teeth!
My mom *wants to* have a picnic.
My dad *doesn't want to* have a picnic.
My brothers *want to* play soccer.
They *don't want to* play volleyball.

Unit 8

Language lab 1

Like/enjoy/love:

Do *you like doing* sports at school?
Yes, I do.
I like doing gymnastics. *I'm good at doing* cartwheels.
He enjoys studying English.
She loves going to the museum. *She doesn't enjoy going* to the mall.
We like going to the playground. *We're good at riding* our bikes.
They love eating carrots.
They don't like swimming.

Language lab 2

Why and Because:

Why do you like going to the playground?
Because I can have fun with my friends.

Why is he studying English?
Because he wants to travel.

Why does she like going to the museum?
Because she likes looking as fossils.

Grammar Reference

Unit 1

Grammar 1

Going to for immediate future (affirmative and negative statements and question form):

She *is going to* buy a book. She *isn't going to* buy a blanket.
He *is going to* go to the market. He *isn't going to* go to the bakery.
They *are going to* buy apples. They *aren't going to* buy mangoes.

Are you *going to* buy some cakes?
No, I'm not.

Are you *going to* meet your friends?
Yes, I am.

Grammar 2

Prepositions of time:

What time are you meeting your friends?
At 11 o'clock.

How long are you going to stay at the mall?
For three hours.

When are you going to go to the supermarket?
On Thursday.

When are you going to go to the mall again?
In a few weeks.

Unit 2

Grammar 1

Comparing the Simple Past and Simple Present (affirmative and negative statements):

She *rides* her bike, she *doesn't take* the bus. She *wears* warm clothes. They all *play* soccer after school. They *don't play* basketball.

She *rode* her bike, she *didn't take* the bus. She *wore* warm clothes. They all *played* soccer after school. They *didn't play* basketball.

Grammar 2

Using *could* and *ago* to talk about abilities in the past:

When *could* you play soccer?
I *could* play soccer when I was six.
That's four years *ago*.

When *could* you ride a bike?
I *couldn't* ride a bike two years *ago*.
I learned to ride a bike last year.

Grammar Reference

Unit 3

Grammar 1

Will for predictions (affirmative and negative statements and question form):

Will we go to school in the future?
No, we *won't* go to school. We *will* study at home. We *won't* sit in a classroom. We *will* study in our bedroom.

Will we have a teacher?
Yes, we *will*.

Will we play sports?
No, we *won't*.

Grammar 2

Will with wh- questions:

When will we study?
We *will* study in the evenings.

How will we communicate with our teacher?
We *will* talk to our teacher on a computer screen.

What will we study?
We *will* study recycling and learn to grow food.

Who will we talk to?
We *will* talk to our friends on weekends.

Where will we meet our friends?
We *will* meet them in the park.

Unit 4

Grammar 1

Past Progressive (affirmative and negative statements and question form):

Yesterday, I *was making* a camp with my friends.
We *were exploring* the forest.
Ali *was cooking*. He *wasn't collecting* leaves.
Maya and Leon *were climbing* trees. They *weren't doing* their homework.
Was Ali *using* a knife?
No, he *wasn't*.
Was he *cooking* rice?
Yes, he *was*.
Were Maya and Leon *wearing* gloves?
Yes, they *were*.
Were they *using* a rope?
No, they *weren't*.

Grammar 2

Simple Past with the Past Progressive:

What *were* you *doing* when it *started* to rain?
I *was swinging* from a tree when it *started* to rain. I *wasn't wearing* a coat!
My friends *were eating* when it *started* to rain. They *weren't cooking*.

Grammar Reference

Unit 5

Grammar 1

First Conditional:

If they *compost* the kitchen waste, it *will rot*.

If they *reuse* glass jars and plastic bottles, there *will be* less waste.

If they *walk or cycle*, there *won't be* as much pollution.

If they *don't recycle*, they *won't protect* the environment.

Grammar 2

More than/Fewer than:

There are *fewer* glass bottles *than* plastic bottles.

There are *more* metal cans *than* paper to recycle.

Are there *more* glass jars *than* shopping bags? Yes, there are.

Are there *fewer* flowers *than* trees? No, there aren't. There are more.

Unit 6

Grammar 1

Should for obligations:

You *should* do your homework.
You *shouldn't* be late for school.
You *should* listen to the teacher.
You *shouldn't* talk in class.

Adverbs of frequency (*always, often, sometimes, never*)

I *always* do my homework.
We *often* practice playing music.
She *sometimes* tidies her bedroom.
He *never* takes out the trash.

Grammar 2

Making suggestions with *Should I …?*/ *Do you want me to …?*:

Should I make lunch?
Yes!

Do you want me to get everyone a drink?
Good idea! It's been a really hot day.

Grammar Reference

Unit 7

Grammar 1

Infinitives of purpose:

We eat ice cream *to keep* us cool.
We wear sunglasses *to protect* our eyes.
We use cream *to stop* the sun burning our skin.

Grammar 2

Talking about illnesses:

My head *hurts*. I have a *headache*.
My back *doesn't hurt*. I don't have a *backache*.
His ear *hurts*. He has an *earache*.

Does your stomach *hurt*?
Yes, it does.

Do you have a *stomachache*?
Yes, I do.

Unit 8

Grammar 1

Talking about the past, present, and future using the Simple Past, Present Progressive, and Future with *will*:

This morning, she *learned* about endangered animals.
She *saw* some rare turtles.
She *is having* a picnic.
She *is drinking* juice and *eating* a sandwich.
After lunch, she *will see* the elephants.
She *won't see* any eagles.

Grammar 2

Expressing feelings (scared *of* …, interested *in* …, worried *about* … excited *about*…):

How about going to see the wolves?
Oh, no! I'm *scared of* wolves.
What about the giraffes?
OK. I'm *interested in* giraffes.
I'm *worried about* the tigers because they are endangered.
I'm *excited about* the bears. They're my favorite animals!

Irregular verbs

	Present Simple	Past Simple
be	I am You are He/She/It is We are They are	I was You were He/She/It was We were They were
be able to	I can You can He/She/It can We can They can	I could You could He/She/It could We could They could
build	I build You build He/She/It builds We build They build	I built You built He/She/It built We built They built
buy	I buy You buy He/She/It buys We buy They buy	I bought You bought He/She/It bought We bought They bought
do	I do You do He/She/It does We do They do	I did You did He/She/It did We did They did
drink	I drink You drink He/She/It drinks We drink They drink	I drank You drank He/She/It drank We drank They drank
eat	I eat You eat He/She/It eats We eat They eat	I ate You ate He/She/It ate We ate They ate

	Present Simple	**Past Simple**
find	I find You find He/She/It finds We find They find	I found You found He/She/It found We found They found
fly	I fly You fly He/She/It flies We fly They fly	I flew You flew He/She/It flew We flew They flew
get	I get You get He/She/It gets We get They get	I got You got He/She/It got We got They got
go	I go You go He/She/It goes We go They go	I went You went He/She/It went We went They went
grow	I grow You grow He/She/It grows We grow They grow	I grew You grew He/She/It grew We grew They grew
have	I have You have He/She/It has We have They have	I had You had He/She/It had We had They had
hit	I hit You hit He/She/It hits We hit They hit	I hit You hit He/She/It hit We hit They hit

Irregular verbs

	Present Simple	Past Simple
know	I know You know He/She/It knows We know They know	I knew You knew He/She/It knew We knew They knew
make	I make You make He/She/It makes We make They make	I made You made He/She/It made We made They made
read	I read You read He/She/It reads We read They read	I read You read He/She/It read We read They read
run	I run You run He/She/It runs We run They run	I ran You ran He/She/It ran We ran They ran
say	I say You say He/She/It says We say They say	I said You said He/She/It said We said They said
see	I see You see He/She/It sees We see They see	I saw You saw He/She/It saw We saw They saw
sleep	I sleep You sleep He/She/It sleeps We sleep They sleep	I slept You slept He/She/It slept We slept They slept

	Present Simple	**Past Simple**
stand	I stand You stand He/She/It stands We stand They stand	I stood You stood He/She/It stood We stood They stood
steal	I steal You steal He/She/It steals We steal They steal	I stole You stole He/She/It stole We stole They stole
take	I take You take He/She/It takes We take They take	I took You took He/She/It took We took They took
throw	I throw You throw He/She/It throws We throw They throw	I threw You threw He/She/It threw We threw They threw
wear	I wear You wear He/She/It wears We wear They wear	I wore You wore He/She/It wore We wore They wore
write	I write You write He/She/It writes We write They write	I wrote You wrote He/She/It wrote We wrote They wrote

OUR WORLD

INTRO:
Here we stand: children of every age,
This is our world and the world's our stage.
We can laugh, we can cry — we can float, we can fly,
We can dance, we can sing — we can do almost anything
in OUR world ... our *beautiful* world.

VERSE 1:
Some of us are small; some of us are tall,
Some of us are shy; some of us say hi to everybody,
Some of us like numbers; some of us love words,
Some of us watch football, and some of us watch the birds!

(CHORUS)
This is *our* world ... we're different but the same.
We live and learn together — we get to know each other ...
in OUR world ... our *beautiful* world.

VERSE 2:
Some of us like music; some of us like cars,
Some of us see pictures, looking at the stars,
Some of us are scientists, trying to find the code,
All of us can help a friend and give a hand to hold.

This is *our* world — there's room for everyone.
We learn to live together, and we have a lot of fun ...
In ***our*** world ... in ***our*** world ... in our beautiful world!

English Code
Level 4

CERTIFICATE

WELL DONE!

_____
Student's Name

_____
Teacher's Signature and Date

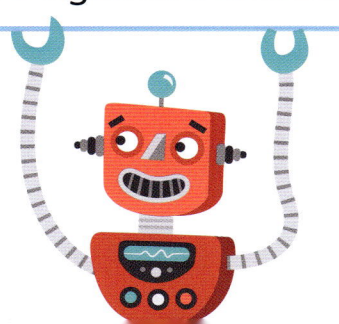

PEARSON

Unit 1
COMMUNICATION

Press-out

My name: _____

I'm going on an adventure vacation in (a) _____ .

I'm going to (b) _____ .

I'm going to arrive on (c) _____ .

I'm going to stay for (d) _____ .

I'm going to get up every day at (e) _____ .

I'm going to (f) _____ and _____ .

My partner's name: _____

_____ is going on an adventure vacation in (a) _____ .

_____ is going to (b) _____ .

_____ is going to arrive on (c) _____ .

_____ is going to stay for (d) _____ .

_____ is going to get up every day at (e) _____ .

_____ is going to (f) _____ and _____ .

Unit 3
COMMUNICATION

Press-out

ON THE SPACE COLONY

1 _____ will you live?

2 _____ will you live with?

3 _____ will you eat?

4 _____ will you wear?

5 _____ will you get oxygen?

6 _____ will you get fuel?

7 _____ will you come back to Earth?

8 _____ will you travel back to Earth?

My answers

1 _____
2 _____
3 _____
4 _____
5 _____
6 _____
7 _____
8 _____

_____'s answers

1 _____
2 _____
3 _____
4 _____
5 _____
6 _____
7 _____
8 _____

Culture 2

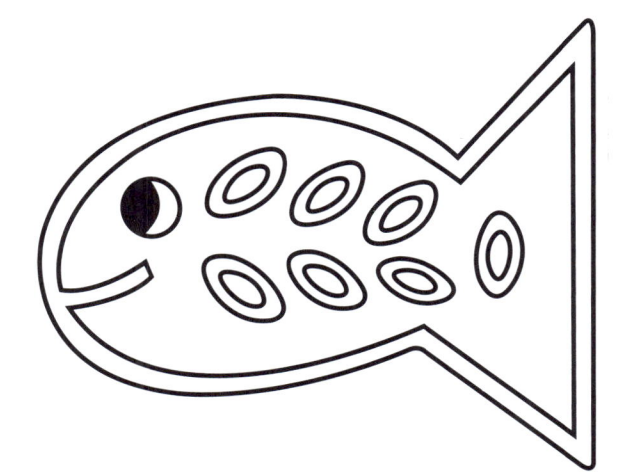

Press-out

Now I can ...

Stickers